The Girls and Boys Book About Good and Bad Behavior

The Girls and Boys Book About Good and Bad Behavior

Richard A. Gardner, M.D.
Clinical Professor of Child Psychiatry
Columbia University
College of Physicians and Surgeons

Illustrations by

Al Lowenheim

Creative Therapeutics
155 County Road, Cresskill, New Jersey 07626-0317

Library of Congress Cataloging-in-Publication Data

Gardner, Richard A.
    The girls and boys book about good and bad behavior / Richard A.
Gardner : illustrations by Al Lowenheim.
        p.   cm.
    Summary: Designed for use by both parents and children, this book
discusses issues affecting desirable human behavior. There are
chapters on self-esteem, pleasure and pain, shame, guilt, sympathy,
and love.
    ISBN 0-933812-21-3
    1. Adjustment (Psychology)—Juvenile literature.   2. Children—
Conduct of life.   [1. Conduct of life.   2. Behavior.]
I. Lowenheim, Al, 1947–   ill.   II. Title.
BF335.G37   1990
155.4'1825—dc20   90–31241
                                                             CIP
                                                              AC

PRINTED IN THE UNITED STATES OF AMERICA
10   9   8   7   6   5   4   3   2   1

To my grandson
David Benjamin Gardner
For the joy you give me

Other Children's Books by Richard A. Gardner

The Boys and Girls Book About Divorce
Dr. Gardner's Stories About the Real World, Volume I
Dr. Gardner's Stories About the Real World, Volume II
Dr. Gardner's Fairy Tales for Today's Children
MBD: The Family Book About Minimal Brain
    Dysfunction
Dr. Gardner's Modern Fairy Tales
The Boys and Girls Book About One-Parent Families
Dorothy and the Lizard of Oz
Dr. Gardner's Fables for Our Times
The Boys and Girls Book About Stepfamilies

Contents

Acknowledgments

When I wrote this book, I could not know beforehand whether children would be receptive to it. My hope, of course, was that they would become deeply absorbed and profit enormously from reading it. My fear, however, was that they would find it boring and would thereby learn little or nothing from it. Accordingly, "with my heart in my mouth" I lent copies to children of friends and relatives as well as child patients—to learn whether it was worthy of publication. Fortunately, most children were enthusiastic, especially those who read the book along with a parent. Furthermore, I found the book especially useful in therapy where the messages served as points of departure for therapeutic interchanges. Parents, especially, were enthusiastic and claimed that I had here a very useful contribution.

My first acknowledgment then is to the children who read this book. In order to preserve the anonymity of those children who were patients, I note here only the first and middle names of all the children (nonpatients included) who provided services in the "field trials."

Amy Cara
Andrew Harten
Bethany Brooke

Jonathan Zev
Joshua Aaron
Julie Ann

Bryan Andrew
Daniella Maxine
David Christian
David Michael
Denton Cooley
Gabrielle Nadine
Howard Jason
Jean Marie
Jed Eric
Jessica Elise

Katelijne Angelique
Matthew John
Michael Joseph
Michael Kaj
Michael Nathaniel
Peter Adrian
Randi Alyson
Rebecca Sarah
Steven Neil
Susan Elizabeth

I wish to express my gratitude, as well, to the parents of these children for their participation and comments. The feedback that I received from both parents and children proved useful in the earlier modifications of the book.

I am indebted to Robert Mulholland for his editing of the manuscript. He provided useful suggestions, yet respected my wishes regarding style, format, and content. I am also grateful for the editorial contributions of Frances S. Dubner.

I am grateful to Donna L. La Tourette for typing the manuscript in its various renditions and for providing useful editorial comments. I am indebted also to Robert Tebbenhoff of Lind Graphics, in Woodcliff Lake, N.J., for his contributions to the production of this book, from manuscript to final volume.

I am deeply indebted to Al Lowenheim whose illustrations complement well the text. Over the 20 years I have known Al, his illustrations have been a valuable contribution to my children's books. Al's drawings add a note of hope and levity to even the grimmest material and enhance immeasurably the attractiveness of my books to child readers. I am fortunate to have him as a collaborator.

Introduction
for Parents,
Teachers,
and Therapists

The Purposes of This Book

This book derives from over 30 years practicing child psychiatry. Psychotherapy, more than anything else, is an educational experience. It involves the correction of distortions about the world that have contributed to the development and perpetuation of the patient's problems. The didactical experience, however, must take place in a setting in which there is a good relationship between the patient and the therapist. Without such a relationship there will be little if any receptivity to the therapist's teaching, little identification with the therapist as a person, and therefore little incorporation by the patient of the messages imparted by the therapist in the context of the treatment.

1

In this book I present some of the most important messages I have attempted to impart to my child patients throughout the course of my career. However, it would be an error for parents to conclude that these communications are only useful for children with psychological problems. Parents need only open to any page in this book and they will find there principles that are important for all children, normal and abnormal, typical and atypical. In fact, I would go further and state that everything herein is applicable to all people, regardless of age. The issues relate to the common problems with which all of us are confronted throughout the course of our lives. Psychiatric disturbance, more than anything else, derives from maladaptive and/or inappropriate solutions to these fundamental problems of life. Accordingly, when we teach these principles to our children early in life, and they become part of their everyday thinking and acting, we can prevent the development of a wide variety of psychological disturbances which result from misinterpretations and inappropriate resolutions of the problems being dealt with here.

An Outline of the Issues
Covered in This Book

The book is divided into eight chapters, each of which deals with an important area of functioning in life—not only how we deal with ourselves, but how we function with others. It begins with a discussion of self-esteem, a central building block of our personality structure. Alfred Adler, one of the early psychoanalytic pioneers, considered problems related to self-esteem to be central to the development of psychological disturbance. He thought that Freud placed too much emphasis on sexual issues and did not give proper attention to the self-esteem factor. I believe that it was unfortunate that Freud prevailed on this issue in that many more psychotherapists were influenced by Freud's teachings than they were by Adler's. But we are not dealing here with a question of either/or. Both sex and self-esteem play an important role in our lives. It was just that Freud's emphasis on sex resulted in a downplaying of the self-esteem issue. Most, if not all, forms of psychological disorder include elements related to self-esteem. Either they represent an attempt to compensate for feelings of low self-worth (a term I use synonymously with self-esteem), or they involve attempts to avoid situations that might lower self-worth. In Chapter One I discuss those factors that are likely to enhance self-esteem, and those that are likely to lower it. Throughout, specific examples are given that enhance the child's ability to make these important distinctions—examples that help children think and behave in ways that are likely to enhance self-worth.

A central problem for society has been that of getting people to behave in ways that are not destructive to its survival. We cannot allow individuals to do wantonly and frivolously whatever they want when they want to. In such a state of anarchy no one is safe; everyone lives in fear of predators and chaos ensues. A central question for humanity has been that of how to get people to comply with the "rules." Probably the earliest methods of "helping people remember" to follow them were the utilization of pleasure and pain, that is, reward and punishment. In Chapter Two I discuss the applicability of these principles to children's behavior at the youngest level.

As the child matures, a more sophisticated method of teaching children to comply with social standards is the utilization of the shame mechanism. Chapter Three focuses on this issue, with particular emphasis on the balance between insufficient and excessive use of the mechanism.

Guilt (Chapter Four), a mental mechanism that is more complex than shame, probably represents a more recent development in the history of humankind. Once guilt is instilled, authorities can relax their vigil—because individuals can then be relied upon to inhibit themselves from engaging in behavior that would be detrimental to the survival of the group. Unfortunately, we in the 20th century still have a long way to go with regard to the optimum utilization of this mechanism. Although the chapter deals with the extremes—too much and too little guilt—I believe we still do not have enough guilt in this world when one looks at the total picture of what is going on today. It is my hope that this chapter will, in an admittedly small way, contribute to a rectification of this problem. The sequential development of pain/pleasure, shame, and guilt in the history of society is reflected in the same sequential development of these in the child.

Chapter Five, Sympathy, deals with the important issue of putting ourselves in other people's positions—another quality necessary for the survival of a society that can justifiably be called civilized. It is no surprise that this capacity is often referred to as the Golden Rule—so central is it to our well being and our ability to live together with one another. Just as there is not enough guilt in this world, there is not enough sympathy. And my hope again is that this chapter might contribute in some way to an alleviation of this problem.

Chapter Six—Stop, Look, Listen, and Think—deals with the problem of impulsivity. When teachers and

4

parents say that a child is not paying attention, they are often referring to weaknesses in this area. We are living at a time when the diagnosis attention-deficit disorder (ADD) is very much in vogue. The presumption is that these children are suffering with some kind of a neurological disturbance. I am in disagreement. The main problem here is that, for the first time in the history of humankind, we are asking children to sit still for six-to-eight hours a day in a classroom and pay attention to the teacher. Prior to this century the vast majority of children were not educated. The boys were primed to serve as warriors, food gatherers, hunters, and protectors. Successful functioning in these realms involved high levels of physical activity and quick action. Those boys who lacked these qualities were not as likely to survive. Boys today are still endowed with this genetic programming—programming that ill equips them to "sit still and listen to the teacher." In contrast, the most desirable girls were those with more sedentary qualities, especially with regard to child-rearing ability. Girls with these qualities were more likely to survive and pass their genetic heritage down to their progeny. Although social and cultural factors (especially in the 20th century) allow and even encourage survival of alternative patterns, not enough time has passed for these patterns to be represented to a significant degree in the genetic pool.

When we place these hunters and warriors in a classroom it is not surprising that they do not sit still and "pay attention" throughout six-to-eight hours of didactics. Girls, being genetically programmed to more sedentary roles, adjust better at the grade-school level, as any elementary school teacher will testify. Those who work with the so-called ADD children agree that the "disorder" is much more common in boys than girls—ratios in the scientific literature ranging from two-to-one to ten-to-one. The fact that certain medications will reduce these children's activity level does not in any way prove that we are dealing here with a sickness. All it does prove is that certain medications will quiet children down and make them more receptive to sitting still for long periods.

Throughout the history of humankind individuals have been confronted with situations in which they had to make immediate decisions regarding whether they should fight or flee. Dangers and enemies were all around. Sometimes fight was the best choice with regard to survival, and sometimes flight. Dealing properly with fight and flight in our more complex society can cause many problems for children. Chapter Seven deals with these issues and provides important guidelines.

Last, Chapter Eight deals with love, a word that has many different meanings and many different utilizations. Here I try to clarify for children some of its important meanings, especially as they relate to feelings about oneself and one's relationships with others.

Values and Ethics

As the reader may by now appreciate, there is much in this book that relates to values and ethics. I use the word values to refer to what a particular culture or society considers to be good and bad, that is, valuable and not valuable. I use the word ethics to refer to one subdivision of values, that is, the things we consider good and bad in our relationships with others, what we consider ethical and unethical. There are therapists who state that their treatment does not involve in any way the imposition of their own values on their patients. This is at best naive and at worst a lie. Therapy involves an attempt to change a person's behavior. If a therapist starts with the assumption that behavior A is inappropriate, unacceptable, or sick (euphemisms for "bad"), that is a value judgment. If the therapist is going to try to change behavior A to behavior B, then that therapist is making the assumption that behavior B is more acceptable, appropriate, and healthy (euphemisms for "good"). All this is inextricably loaded with values. If the therapist believes that substituting the word "sick" for "bad" and the word "healthy" for "good" removes the treatment from the realm of value imposition, then that therapist is very much out of touch with the reality of what is going on in the process.

A mother, for example, brings her seven-year-old boy to a psychiatrist with the complaint that the child has a very high IQ, but is underachieving in school. The teacher complains that the boy is destructive in the classroom, does not pay attention, picks fights with peers, and refuses to do homework. On inquiry, the therapist learns that the parents have serious marital problems, are fighting continually, and often speak of divorce. The therapist learns, as well, that the child is so distracted, upset, and depressed by what is going on in the home that he cannot concentrate on his schoolwork and is acting out his anger in the classroom. The therapist recommends that the child be seen in treatment and that counseling for the parents be provided as well.

This therapist's recommendation is based on his (her) agreement with the parents that education is a healthy or *good* thing, and that anyone who is not taking advantage of one's educational opportunities is doing a sick or *bad* thing. Although I share this therapist's opinion regarding this educational value, it is still a value. There are some people who have little commitment to the educational process or to other societal institutions. Also the therapist's attempts to improve the marital relationship is based on his (her) value that a marriage is better than a divorce. Here again, a value is being imposed upon the parents. This book too, is replete with my own values. I believe that most parents subscribe to most of the values presented herein. I hope, as well, that they agree that imparting these values to their children will be useful to them.

We are living at a time when school systems are reluctant to teach formally values and ethics and are even frightened to do so. One concern is the choice of which values to teach. There is the ever-present fear that any selection will alienate a significant percentage of parents, and so the best solution is to stay away entirely from these "touchy subjects." Accordingly, the teaching of values and ethics has often been confined to parochial schools, much to the loss of children receiving a public education. I think this is an unfortunate situation. I believe that most of the values of most of the religions are very similar. I believe that this book presents such values. I find it hard to imagine parents objecting to teaching their children about the Golden Rule, sympathy, self-control, appropriate and healthy shame and guilt, and love. One of my hopes, then, is that the material contained herein might serve as guidelines for public (and, if necessary, parochial) school programs in which values and ethics are taught.

Is Using the Word "Bad" Really So Bad?

I suspect that some parents, and probably many more therapists, are somewhat surprised about the

8

title of this book: *The Girls and Boys Book About Good and Bad Behavior.* We are living at a time when allegedly sophisticated and sensitive parents strictly refrain from using the word *bad.* Many will self-righteously say: "I would never use that word to *my* child." And therapists warn that the utilization of this word may result in severe damage to children's self-esteem. In order to protect children from the presumably detrimental effects of the use of the word *bad,* many therapists will advise parents to separate the unacceptable deed from the person who performed it. When Billy spills his milk, whether accidentally or purposely, one should not say, "Billy, you spilled the milk." Rather, one should say, "The milk spilled." In this way the child and the act are separated. Presumably, it was not the child who spilled the milk. It was something to do with the hand and the milk, somewhat remote from the brain of the child. This is absurd. The implication is that the hand acted independently of the brain and the rest of Billy's body. Billy's hand committed the bad act, not Billy.

To say to a child (in a moderately irritated way), "Why don't you watch what you're doing? You just spilled the milk. That's a bad thing to do. Now I want you to help me clean it up"—is a perfectly acceptable and even judicious way of dealing with the situation. One is not saying or even implying: "You're so bad that every cell of your body is rotten. You'll be an outcast from society and I can't imagine how anyone will ever want to have contact with you for the rest of your life." The latter statement, obviously, is likely to lower feelings of self-worth. The former is merely saying to the child that at that particular point he (she) did something that was a bad act and that a good act in rectification, such as cleaning up the mess, will wipe the slate clean. It is hoped that the negative feedback of the irritated parent will serve as a deterrent to recurrences and the discomforts of the rectification process (cleaning up the mess) will also help the child remember not to spill the milk again.

Furthermore, children are often confused by messages that try to separate the deed from the doer. Deep down they know full well that what they did was bad, and that their brains control their hands. As they get older they are likely to recognize the absurdity of such parental comments. And this cannot but compromise the parent-child relationship. Accordingly, I have no problem with the title of this book and I believe that children will have no problem with it either.

The Age Range for Which This Book Is Designed

This book is designed to be read by children who have reached about the third to fourth grade level of reading comprehension. Younger children (down to about age six) will understand much when read to. Some in this younger age bracket enjoy reading what they can, while parents assist with words they have not yet mastered. Although this is not a fun book in the traditional sense, it is designed to be attractive to a child. Its lure comes from the fact that the issues discussed in it are of vital interest to children. It has been my experience that when such issues are presented in the manner used here, children will often become intensely curious. Their interest and absorption is derived from their appreciation that the topics being discussed are the very ones that have been causing them much concern and even grief. Furthermore, the Alfred Lowenheim illustrations have proved to enhance even further children's involvement in the material. Last, the descriptive vignettes, which are designed to enhance the efficacy of my messages, serve as a balance to the heavier, more didactic material. But they also add levity and excitement which enhance the child's involvement in the book.

Adolescents can also benefit from this book, although they may exhibit some hesitation at the prospect of reading it. They may consider it to be beneath them because it is written at the third to fourth grade level. In addition, the cartoon illustrations may also remind them of books for younger children. The messages provided here, however, are for all ages. Accordingly, there is much that adolescents can profit from if they can be encouraged to overcome their initial resistance. Parents, as well, will immediately recognize that I am also writing for them. Adolescents observing their parents reading the book may well overcome these early reservations.

Interestingly, many parents who read the original manuscript versions with their children informed me that they themselves had learned much from the book and considered it a book for adults as well—even though written to be read by children. I was pleased to learn this because the adult audience is generally in my mind when I write my children's books. It has always been my hope that the messages contained in these books will not only serve children well in their childhood but remain useful for them throughout the course of their lives.

How This Book Should Be Used

This book is not simply designed for the child to read alone. Rather, it is also my hope that children and their parents will read this book together. In fact, my experience with the manuscripts of this book that were given out to children prior to its publication led me to the firm conclusion that for many children, especially younger ones, this book can be heavy reading. Accordingly, it *requires* parental enticement. This is especially true of Chapter One, which may be somewhat "heavy" reading for some children but serves as a foundation for the rest of the book. But even for older children reading the book together with the child is often necessary. Most parents have agreed, however, that the efforts to overcome initial reluctance were well worth the effort. It is important that the child *and* parents talk about the issues raised in the book as points of departure for meaningful discussion. This may not only serve to alleviate the problems being discussed, but should help to bring parent and child closer. Repetition is an extremely important element in the learning process. And this is even more true for children than adults. Accordingly, it may be necessary to discuss repeatedly many of the issues raised herein if they are to become incorporated into the child's psychic structure and thereby affect behavior on an ongoing basis.

This book was not designed to be read in one sitting. No child (and, in fact, no parent) could be expected to absorb all its contents at once. It is best read in short segments, in order to provide the child the opportunity to become comfortable with advice that may be difficult to comprehend or implement. It is desirable that the chapters be read in the sequence in which they are presented, because the earlier chapters serve as a foundation for the later ones. Furthermore, words are defined the first time they are used, and if the book is not read in sequence the child will be deprived of important definitions—necessary to the understanding of the book. However, once the child has completed the book it serves well as a "reference" to be returned to for reiteration and further discussion.

This book is best read when the child is relaxed and comfortable. A competing television program or the distracting sounds of other children playing will not provide the proper atmosphere for the child to comprehend and absorb the book's contents. Bedtime has traditionally been the time for children's reading, both alone and with a parent. If the child is still quite alert, bedtime would be a good time for reading this book, but the sleepy child is not likely to gain much from reading it at that time.

Parents will know that they are using this book successfully by the child's interest in reading it (alone or with the parent) and by the child's receptivity to discussing its messages. Such discussions not only entrench its important issues but deepen the parent-child bond as well—and this may be one of the most important benefits of this book.

Additional Comments for Teachers

As mentioned, schools (even public institutions) have an excellent opportunity to teach values and ethics and this may be done without offending individual religious beliefs. It is my hope, therefore, that this book will enjoy widespread popularity in school systems. I have already mentioned how many children—especially younger ones—need to be enticed into reading this book. Teachers have a wonderful opportunity to provide such "encouragement" by specifically assigning homework material. It is crucial that such assignments begin with the first chapter and then proceed through the course of the book, chapter by chapter. Although the whole book rests on the first chapter as its foundation, many of the chapters require reading previous ones if the child is to appreciate optimally what is being read. Teachers also have a wonderful opportunity to use the book for classroom reading and then utilize what has been read as points of departure for classroom discussion.

Additional Comments for Therapists

Although written primarily for children and their parents, this book (as I am sure is obvious to many) was also written with therapists in mind. As mentioned, psychological disturbances are derived from maladaptive ways of dealing with the fundamental problems of life with which all of us are confronted. And therapy, more than anything else, is an attempt to correct inappropriate methods of dealing with these problems. The book, in a sense, can be viewed as a form of preventive psychiatry in that its proper utilization should contribute to the prevention of the development of many types of psychological disorder. However, if such disturbances are present, the information in these pages can be of definite therapeutic benefit—both within and outside of the consultation room.

Therapists should find parts (if not all) of it useful in the course of the therapeutic session. When a topic comes up in treatment that is relative to material in this book (a very common occurrence) the therapist might take out the book and read along with the child the pertinent sections. And this material can then become a point of departure for further discussions. This book can also be used as a "homework assignment"—again in a piecemeal fashion. The therapist does well to discuss in a subsequent session with the child what has been previously read. The therapist should also encourage the patient's parents to read the book along with the child and to use the material as a point of departure for family discussions. Such discussions not only serve the immediate purposes of the treatment (with regard to imparting important information to the child) but also strengthen the parent-child bond. And this cannot but be therapeutic. Then the material should be related directly to the child's problems. Therapists generally appreciate the importance of reiteration and will not expect the child to change behavior on the basis of one reading and a single subsequent discussion. However, my experience has been that with repetition the book's messages are likely to be incorporated into the child's psychic structure and will contribute thereby to the alleviation of symptoms.

Final Comments

In closing, I would like to emphasize to the reader that I could not have written this book over 30 years ago when I first began practicing child psychiatry. Although written to be read by children, it contains many important principles of living that are often not appreciated by many adults (including therapists). One should not be deceived, then, by its ostensible simplicity. Yet, these principles are not so difficult to understand that the average youngster in mid-childhood could not comprehend my messages. It is my hope that the benefits that I have personally derived from the information in this volume will prove useful to children and their parents in both the prevention and alleviation of psychological disorder. If successful in this regard, it should contribute to the betterment of their sense of well-being and an enhanced ability to appreciate and enjoy their lives.

Introduction for Girls and Boys

How do you do, girls and boys? My name is Dr. Richard Gardner. I am a psychiatrist. Some of you may not know what a psychiatrist is. A psychiatrist is a kind of doctor who **tries** to help people with their troubles, worries, and problems. It is important to remember that I have only said that the psychiatrist **tries** to help people with their troubles, worries, and problems. Sometimes psychiatrists can help people with their problems, and sometimes they can't. Whether or not they can help depends upon the person who is coming for help. The more the person tries to help himself or herself, the better the chances the psychiatrist will be able to help that person feel better. If the person doesn't listen to what the psychiatrist says and doesn't try to do the kinds of things the psychiatrist thinks are good

17

to do, the person will probably not be helped with the problems. It is for this reason that a psychiatrist cannot promise to help; the psychiatrist can only promise to try.

I am also a special kind of psychiatrist. I am a child psychiatrist. That means that I have learned how to try to help children with their special kinds of problems (that grownups might not have). But psychiatrists aren't the only ones who have learned how to try to help people with worries. There are also, for example, psychologists, social workers, and counselors. All these kinds of people who try to help those with their troubles are called psychotherapists. Often, people will just say *therapist* when they mean *psychotherapist*. And that is what I will do in this book because it's easier to say.

It is important to remember that everyone in the whole wide world has—at times—troubles, worries, or

problems. It is normal to have some. No one has ever gone through life without having some worries.

But this does **not** mean that everyone should see a therapist. The only people who should see a therapist are those who have not been able to solve their problems themselves or with the help of other people, such as parents and friends. These people may have such big problems, or so many troubles, that they have to get help from a therapist.

This book is for **all** children. It is for those who have the normal problems of life. And it is for those who have so many problems that they should see a therapist. Both kinds of children should find the information here useful. My hope is that this book will help normal children have fewer problems. My hope also is that it will help children who do see a therapist get better faster. For both kinds of children I hope that they will read carefully what I say here, think hard about what they have read, and try to do the things that I suggest in it. I believe that those children who do these things will feel better about themselves, and get along better with their friends, parents, teachers, and other people. I believe then that they will have happier lives.

It is important to remember that some of the things that I say here may be hard to understand. If you read the book slowly and carefully you will understand it better. Also, it is not necessary to read the whole book at once. Most children read only a little at a time. It is much better to read this book along with a parent. This is especially true for younger children. If you try to read the book alone you may find some of it hard to under-

stand. Therefore, it is very important to read this book with one or both of your parents.

This book is not only written to be read. It is also written to be spoken about. Therefore, it is very important to discuss the things you read in it with other people, especially your parents. Also, parents can help you understand the hard parts. But even if you understand everything in the book, it is still a good idea to talk about these things with other people. And, if you are in therapy, it is a very good idea to talk about these things with your therapist. This is especially true if something in it gets you upset, scared, or angry.

Of course, children who have not yet learned to read—or who only read a little bit—cannot read this book by themselves. Such children will still understand much that is in this book if they will listen carefully while a parent is reading the book to them. For such children, it is even more important that they talk with their parents about the things being read—to be sure that they understand them.

If you read this book carefully, think about the things I have said in it, and try to do the things I suggest, I believe you will feel better about any problems you may have—whether or not you are in therapy.

CHAPTER 1

Self-Esteem

WHAT IS SELF-ESTEEM?

Self-esteem is what you think about yourself. It is also called self-worth. The two words mean the same thing. Self-esteem is what you **really** think about yourself **inside** when you are all alone. It is not what you try to show all the other people.

HIGH AND LOW SELF-WORTH

If you most often feel good about yourself, and like yourself a lot, then you have high self-esteem. If, however, you **often** feel bad about yourself and don't like yourself very much, then you have low self-esteem. The word **often** is very important here. Nobody has such high self-worth that he or she feels good about himself or herself all the time. Even people with the highest self-worth feel bad about themselves at times. And people with low self-worth do not feel bad about themselves all the time. Even people with the lowest self-worth feel good about themselves at times. So everybody is a mixture. People with high self-worth have more feelings of high self-esteem than low self-esteem. And people with low self-worth have more feelings of low self-esteem than high self-esteem.

HOW TO CHANGE LOW
SELF-ESTEEM
INTO HIGH SELF-ESTEEM

Many of you may be wondering now what people with low self-esteem can do to make themselves feel better, to give them feelings of high self-worth. I am sorry to tell you that there is no simple answer to that question. There is no easy and quick thing you can do to change low self-worth to high self-worth. It often takes a lot of time and many things have to be done. This is because there are many parts to self-esteem.

What You Do and
How You Act

One important part of self-worth relates to what you do and how you act. If you are good, and do good things most of the time, you will feel good about yourself deep down inside. At those times your self-esteem will be high. For example, Mary studied very hard and got very high grades on her report card. She was quite excited and couldn't wait to get home to tell her parents. She was very proud of herself and her

parents were proud of her also. Mary then had high feelings of self-worth. Her parents' being proud of her also increased Mary's feelings of high self-esteem. And that is another part of self-worth, namely, what important people think about you will affect your self-worth.

However, if you do bad things—especially very often—then you will feel bad about yourself most of the time and your self-esteem will be low. For example, Bob cheated on a test in school. He copied the answers from the girl sitting in front of him—a girl who was a very good student. When the teacher returned the test, Bob got a high mark. Bob could not enjoy the high mark. He knew in his heart that he didn't deserve it. He didn't get the feeling of high self-worth that he would have felt had he been honest and earned the high grade himself. He only felt low self-worth because he knew in

his heart that he had cheated. He was also afraid that the girl from whom he cheated might be angry at him, and this too lowered his feelings of self-worth.

Some Examples of Things You Can Do That Will Increase Your Self-worth

There are many things that people can do to increase self-worth. These are the things that most people, especially adults, think are good to do. For example, being nice to your parents, behaving well in school, sharing, treating others nicely, and giving people presents makes others feel good and can make people feel good about themselves. Doing these things increases self-worth. Helping the sick, giving money to the poor, and forgiving people who do bad things are some of the other ways that can increase a person's self-esteem. The older the person is, the more chances a person has to do good things that can increase self-esteem.

Some Examples of Things People Do That Lower Self-worth

There are many things children do which can lower their feelings of self-worth. Some of these things are lying, stealing, and cheating. Some other examples of things that lower self-esteem are not doing jobs around the house, acting like a baby, not sharing, not doing homework, breaking things, and hitting little children. Children who do these things not only feel bad about themselves, but they are made to feel worse when others find out about the bad things they have done.

Tom's behavior was a good example of how what a person does can lower self-worth. Tom was a "sore loser." When he lost a game he would get very upset. Sometimes, he would call the winner bad names and would even have temper tantrums. Once, when he was playing baseball, he dropped a ball that was hit to him by a player on the other team. Instead of mumbling and grumbling, he had a big fit. He jumped around and screamed. The other players, as well as those who were

watching the game, thought that there was something wrong with Tom, and there really was. He was not a good sport. When he realized what a fool he had made of himself and what other people thought of him, he really felt bad about himself.

And adults who do bad things may also feel low self-worth. Victor was a crook. He owned a gun and he held up storekeepers. Once, in the middle of such a robbery, he actually shot a storekeeper who didn't want to give him money. Fortunately, the man wasn't killed. Fortunately also, the police caught Victor and the judge and jury decided that he should go to jail for 20 years. Victor really felt very bad about himself when

the judge told him that he would have to spend so much time in jail.

Good Fun and Bad Fun

There are two kinds of fun: good fun and bad fun. Good fun increases self-esteem, that is, it helps make self-esteem higher. Bad fun decreases self-esteem, that is, it makes self-esteem go lower. Some examples of good fun are sports, playing games, dancing, and singing. Some examples of bad fun are teasing other people, picking on others, laughing at someone who lost a game, and playing funny tricks on other people—tricks that hurt or harm.

For example, Myra went to day camp during her summer vacation. She enjoyed herself very much and had a lot of good fun. She made many good friends and did many fun things together with them. At the beginning of the camp season, everyone was told that there was going to be a big play for the parents at the end of the summer. The directors of the camp asked who wanted to be in the play. However, they warned everybody in advance that although being in the play might be fun, a lot of hard work was involved. Myra tried out for a part and got it. She was very happy. Some of the children who tried out didn't get parts. Although Myra felt sorry for those who didn't get parts in the play, she felt happy that she got one and her self-esteem got higher.

Throughout the summer there was a lot of hard work preparing for the big play to be given at the end. She had to practice dancing and learn songs. She had to spend a lot of time practicing the words to her part. There was much work to be done.

Finally, the big day came. Everyone was very excited. All the parents came. The auditorium was packed. When the play was over everyone in the audience clapped very hard and even cheered. When it was all over Myra's parents said to her that she had done "beautifully" and that they were both very proud of her. But most important, Myra was proud of herself for what she had done. And this increased her feelings of

self-worth. Also, she had done many good, fun things in the play—acting, singing, and dancing—that also increased her feelings of self-esteem.

There are many other kinds of good fun: baking a cake or cookies with a parent, learning how to do card tricks, doing well at a computer game, building models, and wearing costumes. All these things can increase self-worth.

Bad fun lowers feelings of self-worth. Jim, for example, thought it was great fun to put his foot out and trip other children as they passed him in the classroom. One day his teacher saw him doing this to Gail. When Gail fell down she scraped her knees and almost hit her head against the edge of someone's desk. The teacher, Mrs. Rodriguez, came over immediately and said to Jim, "You just did a terrible thing. What

you did could be very dangerous. I know you think that what you just did was fun. To me it's just the opposite. To me it's a terrible, cruel thing. Now wipe that silly smile off your face and go directly down to the principal's office!" So, what started out as a fun thing, something that Jim thought would make him feel better about himself, ended up with his feeling worse about himself. And that's how it is with bad fun. At the beginning it may seem like it's going to make people feel better about themselves; but it ends up with their feeling worse about themselves.

Taking drugs or alcohol is another example of bad fun. Most people who do these stupid things usually start when they are teenagers or a little older. There are some people, however, who actually start to do these things when they are younger than teenagers. Drugs

and alcohol may make a person feel good at the beginning. And many even say that they increase a person's self-esteem. And this is sometimes true when the drug or alcohol is still inside the person's body, before it is used up. But it's not true after the drug or alcohol is used up by the body. Then the person feels very bad and self-esteem gets very low.

There are some people who take drugs and alcohol so often that they cannot go without them. These people go around as if they were always hungry to take drugs or alcohol. Such people are called **addicts**. We say that they are "hooked" and they keep thinking about alcohol or drugs all the time. Such people will often even lie and steal in order to get enough money to buy the drugs or alcohol. And, as I have mentioned, such behavior only makes people feel worse about themselves. Adults may spend every cent they have in order to buy the alcohol or drugs. And being poor all the time also lowers feelings of self-worth. I hope that you never do such a stupid thing as taking drugs or alcohol. Doing so **always** lowers self-esteem.

Good Competition and
Bad Competition

Competition is like a contest. When there is competition each person tries to do something better than the others. Sports is a very good example of a kind of competition. Most often there are two teams and each team tries to do better than the other. Games are another example of competition in which each person tries to win. Winning in a competition can increase feelings of self-worth. However, this will only happen if the person has played fairly, has not cheated, and does not wish to make the people on the other side feel bad about themselves. That is what I call good competition. People who compete this way will feel good about themselves when they win.

In bad competition, a player will cheat or lie, does not follow the rules, and enjoys making the people on the losing side feel bad about themselves. People like that do not feel good about themselves after they win and so winning does not increase their self-esteem. They know inside that they have cheated or lied or that they have not followed the rules. And so they know that the winning wasn't so great. Also, they are so interested in making the other people feel bad that they don't get the pleasure of having won.

Another kind of bad competition relates to "sore losers." These are people who take a game too seriously. They think that if they lose the game that it is the end of the world for them. These are people who think that a loser is a low-life type person. Such people may have fits and tantrums when they lose. This makes them look foolish to other people and all this cannot but lower self-esteem.

George's school had a "spelling bee." A spelling bee is a contest to see who is the best speller. First, there was a contest in each classroom to find out who was the best speller in that class. Then, everyone met in the school auditorium where the best spellers in each class had a contest to see who was going to be the best speller in the school. George studied very hard. Also, he asked his parents and his older sister to practice with him. He got to be such a good speller that he spelled better than most children two or three grades older than himself. Finally, George won the big

spelling bee in the school auditorium. The principal gave him a silver cup, called a trophy. George was very proud of himself. Also, when he got off the stage, he shook the hands of each of the other children who were competing with him for the prize. He even felt a little sorry for those who lost; but he still was happy that he had won. George showed good sportsmanship. He is a good example of good competition. The contest made him work harder and he learned more words. And all this helped George have a feeling of high self-worth.

Betsy was a very good dancer. She started going to dancing school on her third birthday. At that time she went twice a week. By the time she was five, she was going three times a week and her mother would make her practice on other days as well. Betsy's mother and father were always boasting to everybody about what a great dancer Betsy was. And Betsy used to brag too about how good she was. It certainly was true that Betsy was a very good dancer. However, the other children in her class and their parents soon got tired of all this boasting. Soon, the other children started calling her a "show-off." Also, Betsy used to laugh at the other children when they made mistakes and this got them even angrier. Although being a good dancer raised Betsy's self-esteem, not being liked by all the other children in the dance class lowered her self-esteem. But Betsy was doing things that caused the others not to like her. By boasting, being a "show-off," and laughing at others when they made mistakes, she made the others angry. Had she not done these things they would have admired her, wished that they could dance as well as she, and this would have raised her self-esteem. It was sad for Betsy that she didn't know the difference between good competition and bad competition.

Self-Esteem and Self-Assertion

Self-assertion means sticking up for your rights. People who assert themselves properly do not let others take advantage of them. They also do not take advantage of other people. They insist upon getting what they think is right for them to have; but they also respect other people's rights. People who assert themselves in the right way usually have high self-esteem.

There are two wrong ways to assert yourself. One wrong way is to assert yourself too much and always want others to do things your way. People who behave this way do not respect the rights of others. Such people are not liked and even hated. They have few if any friends. This results in low self-esteem and loneliness.

The other wrong way is not to assert oneself enough. People who have this problem often let other people take advantage of them. They don't stand up for their rights. This causes them to be very angry. But they often keep their anger inside and it just sits there and rumbles. It's like the lava and rocks in a volcano before it explodes. Or it's like boiling water trying to get out of a bottle with a cork in it. Bottled-up anger causes feelings of low self-esteem. In Chapter Seven I will talk more about anger and the right and wrong ways of using it.

The right way to assert yourself is in the middle of the two wrong ways, that is, not too much and not too little self-assertion. People who assert themselves properly often have many friends and high feelings of self-worth.

Feeling That You Have to Be Perfect

Most people know that no one is perfect and that everybody has things they are good at as well as things they are bad at. There are some people, however, who believe that it may be okay for others to have bad parts or things they are not good at, but they will not accept the fact that they have weaknesses themselves. They do not want to believe that they themselves are not perfect. Such people, then, may suffer with feelings of low self-worth. They may feel good about themselves when they are not making any mistakes at all. However, when they do make a mistake—even one little mistake—they feel terrible. They feel like failures. They think that they should be so good at everything that they don't make any mistakes at all. Because everybody makes a mistake at times, these people very often suffer with feelings of low self-worth even though they may be doing things quite well.

Marcia, for example, was a very good student. You would think that she would be happy because she was getting high grades in school. However, she kept thinking that the only good mark to get on a test was a perfect score. If she got less than an 'A' she would get very upset. Even an 'A-' would cause her to have crying fits. She would look at the few mistakes that she had

made and would say such things as, "How could I be so stupid?" or "What an idiot I am." As a result, Marcia had feelings of low self-esteem, even though she did very well in school.

And the same thing would happen to Marcia when she would make mistakes when practicing the piano, or when she wouldn't get the ball in the basket when she was playing basketball. She just couldn't accept the fact that no one is perfect and that everyone makes mistakes. She felt that she should somehow be better than others and that she was too good a person to make mistakes, like other people. And this too caused her to have feelings of low self-worth. And this was sad for Marcia because she was really so good at so many things.

There are some people with this problem who often don't try at all, because they fear they will not succeed or be perfect. By doing very little, they accomplish very little so their self-esteem is very low. If they were to try, they would often do well—but certainly not always—and their self-esteem would be higher. Therefore, such people are making a very big mistake.

Covering Up Feelings of Low Self-Worth

All of us cover up, at times, our feelings of low self-esteem. Most of us don't like to admit to others that we have done things that we are ashamed of and make us feel bad about ourselves. That's normal. But there are some people who have very low feelings of self-worth who put on a big show for everybody. They keep telling everyone how great they are and show off a lot. They try to get everybody to think that they are big shots. They boast and even lie. They make little things into big deals. These people really have low self-worth, but try to cover it up. They are being phony. They would like to believe that everyone believes their stories. But this usually doesn't work. Some people may think that such braggers are hot stuff, but most people are turned off and don't want to have much to do with

such boasters. Sooner or later everyone catches on and realizes that the person is full of bull.

So acting like a big shot just doesn't work to make people with low self-esteem feel better about themselves. Deep down inside they know that they are phonies. When all alone they know the truth and then feel bad about themselves.

False Pride and True Pride

Being proud of yourself is called pride. A boy who is a good soccer player has pride in his ability to play soccer. A girl who plays the violin well has pride in herself because of her accomplishment. There are

many other things children can do which can make them feel proud of themselves: making someone a birthday card, keeping your room clean and neat, and being kind to other people. These are examples of **true pride**. True pride increases self-esteem.

The opposite of true pride is **false pride**. When a person tries to feel proud about something that is not really difficult to do, that is false pride. For example, a girl who feels proud of herself because her father is rich is showing false pride. There is nothing that she has done to earn her father's money; so she, herself, has nothing to be proud of. Her father, however—if he earned his money honestly and worked hard—has something to be proud of. If, however, he just got the money from his own father, that is, the girl's grandfather, then he has little or nothing to be proud of. He didn't work to get the money, and so it was no accomplishment for him. Also, if he stole the money or got it by cheating other people, then he also has nothing to be proud of.

Some people say that they're proud to be Americans or are proud that they were born in a certain country. This is nothing to be proud of. They are no better or worse than people who are born in other countries. This is another example of false pride. People, however, who have come to a new country, learned a new language, and passed a test to become citizens of the new country, have something to be proud of. These people have true pride.

In this book I will be saying many other things about good and bad behavior and the things that can help people feel better about themselves. I will also be talking about the things that people might do which could make them feel worse about themselves.

IMPORTANT THINGS
TO REMEMBER

1. Self-esteem is what you really think and feel about yourself, deep inside, when you are all alone. If you like yourself very much, most of the time, you have high self-esteem. If you don't like yourself very much, most of the time, you have low self-esteem.

2. People who do good things feel good about themselves, and have high self-esteem.

3. People who do bad things feel bad about themselves, and have low self-esteem.

4. Everybody is a mixture of high and low self-esteem. Self-esteem is high when the person does more good things than bad things. Self-esteem is low when the person does more bad things than good things.

5. Good fun raises self-esteem. Bad fun lowers self-esteem.

6. Good competition raises self-esteem. Bad competition lowers self-esteem.

7. If you feel that you always have to be perfect, you'll lower your self-esteem.

8. Making believe you have high self-esteem, when you really have low self-esteem, doesn't work. Doing that will only make your self-esteem lower.

9. True pride is being proud of something that you did yourself, that was hard to do, and took a long time. False pride is being proud of something that you didn't have to work hard to accomplish. True pride increases self-esteem. False pride lowers self-esteem.

CHAPTER 2

Pleasure and Pain

PLEASURE

When I use the word **pleasure,** I am talking about the good and enjoyable thoughts and feelings a person may have. There are pleasurable **thoughts** and pleasurable **feelings**. A pleasurable thought, for example, would be thinking about eating ice cream. Thoughts are mainly in the mind. A pleasurable feeling is mainly in the body. Eating ice cream gives you a pleasurable feeling. It is mainly in the body, not just in the mind.

But things are not that simple. A thought can cause a feeling in your body. When you think about ice cream, you also get a little bit of a pleasurable feeling. When you actually eat ice cream you not only think

45

about it, but you also get a much bigger pleasurable feeling.

PAIN

Pain is the opposite of pleasure. When I use the word **pain** I am talking about the bad and hurtful thoughts and feelings a person may have. There are painful thoughts and painful feelings. Painful thoughts are in the mind. A painful thought, for example, would be thinking about falling off a skateboard.

A painful feeling is in the body. Actually falling off

the skateboard and hurting your backside produces a painful feeling. It is in the body, not just in the mind.

But things are not that simple. A thought can cause a feeling. When you think of falling off a skateboard you also get a little bit of a painful feeling. If you actually fall off a skateboard, you get a much bigger painful feeling. But you also have some painful thoughts along with the painful feeling.

When a baby is cuddled and hugged, its body feels very good.

When a baby is left alone and people don't pay attention to it, it feels sad and lonely and will cry.

PLEASURE, PAIN, AND BEHAVIOR

Pleasure and pain have a lot to do with behavior. In fact, the younger the child, the more the parents have

to use **body** pleasure and pain to teach a child about good and bad behavior. Because very young children can't understand many words, the parents have to use body pleasure to help the child learn what's good. And sometimes they even have to use body pain to help a child learn what's bad.

Learning from Pleasurable Feelings

Tom was very good. He picked up all his toys and put them in his toy box. He didn't leave them all over the floor. This made his mother very happy and proud of him. Whenever he was good and put away all his toys, she gave him a big hug and kiss. This made him feel very good all over. These good feelings also helped Tom remember to do good things again. When he was

trying to decide whether or not to do a good thing he would think about his mother's hugging him and he would then decide to do the good thing, like picking up all his toys and putting them in the toy box.

Learning from Painful Feelings

Bobby did a bad thing. While walking down the street with his mother, he suddenly pulled away from her and ran into the street. He was running toward a car that was going very fast. His mother ran after him, grabbed his arm and shouted: "Bobby! Watch out!" The mother caught Bobby just in time. Had she not acted quickly, Bobby would probably have been hit by the car. She then pulled him back to the sidewalk

where they were both safe. By that time Bobby was crying, and his arm was hurting.

If Bobby's mother had only said quietly, "Don't do that again, you might get hit by a car" he would not have understood. He was too young to understand that if you walk into the street you might get hit by a car and might even be killed. But his mother's screaming and his painful arm helped him remember not to do that again. Even though young children can't think very much or understand very much, pain helps them remember not to do again bad or wrong things.

After that Bobby didn't run into the street again. He did **not** stop himself because he really understood that he might get hit by a car. He **did** stop himself because he was afraid that if he did run into the street again his mother might grab him, hurt his arm, and scream at him. These painful thoughts and feelings helped him remember not to run into the street again.

PARENTS' LOVING FEELINGS AND BEHAVIOR

When parents show loving feelings toward a child, the child feels good, pleasurable feelings all over. And when parents hold back their loving feelings—as when they are angry at a child—the child has painful feelings, such as sadness and loneliness. Such painful feelings can also help a child learn right from wrong.

Thinking About Getting Love Helps You to Remember to Be Good

Sara was very good all day. She helped her mother take care of her little baby brother, Adam. She helped

her mother clean up the house. And she helped her mother shop at the supermarket.

At the end of the day her mother said: "I'm very proud of you. You were very helpful to me all day long. You helped with the shopping. You helped me with the baby. And you helped clean the house. It's wonderful to have such a daughter. As soon as Daddy comes home I'm going to tell him about how good you were." She then gave Sara a big hug and a kiss. Sara felt great! Sara felt proud of herself. Also, her self-esteem was

then very high because she had done good things. Her self-esteem was also high because her mother was proud of her. But, most important, she was proud of herself. All these good feelings helped Sara remember to be good again, because she knew that if she was good she would get more of these pleasurable feelings.

Being Afraid of Losing Love
Helps You Remember Not to Be Bad

On another day, however, Sara was just the opposite. She was very naughty. She spilled her milk and blamed it on her brother, who really didn't do it. In fact, he was sleeping in his room when it happened. Her mother said she was lying. Then Sara wouldn't help

her mother clean up the mess. Also, she wouldn't help her mother take care of the baby. And, when they went shopping, she kept putting things in the cart that her mother didn't want to buy. She did this while her mother wasn't looking. So later, when her mother had to pay for everything, these extra things were in the basket, things she didn't need or want. When they got

home her mother was even angrier when she saw that she had bought things that she really didn't need or want.

At the end of the day, her mother said to her: "Sara, I can't stand it any more. From the minute you got up this morning you've been giving me a hard time. I don't know what's gotten into you today. I just can't wait until your father comes home so he can take care of you. I've just got to get away from you and get some peace and quiet." Sara's mother still loved her, but she was so angry then that the loving feelings got covered up by her anger.

While her mother was yelling at her, Sara felt very sad and began to cry. Sadness is a very painful feeling. Her self-worth got lowered because she had done bad things. Her self-esteem also got lowered because her

mother was angry at her. However, these painful thoughts and feelings helped Sara remember to be good. The thought of her mother screaming at her helped her to be good. The thought of her mother hugging and kissing her once again also helped her to be good.

And this is the way that both pleasurable and painful feelings help children remember to be good. They want to avoid the pain of the painful feelings they have when they're bad, and they want to enjoy the pleasure of the pleasurable feelings they have when they're good.

IMPORTANT THINGS TO REMEMBER

1. Very young children don't understand many things.

2. One thing that helps them remember to be good is the pleasure they get when they are good.

3. One thing that helps them remember not to be bad is the painful feelings they get when they are bad.

4. The more good things you do, the more loving feelings you will get from others—especially your parents. Then you will feel good feelings about yourself and your self-worth will get higher.

5. The more bad things you do, the more angry feelings you will get from other people, especially your parents. Then you will feel bad about yourself and your self-worth will get lower.

6. In this way pain and pleasure help children remember to be good and not to be bad. And this is especially true of very young children who do not understand much about the world.

CHAPTER 3

Shame

WHAT IS SHAME?

Shame is a special kind of feeling of low self-esteem. To feel shame two things must happen. First, you must do or say something that you know is wrong or bad. And second, people who are important to you—like your parents, for example—must see you doing the bad thing or learn that you have done it. When these people see you doing the bad thing, you feel ashamed of yourself. And when you think about how disappointed these people are with you—because of the bad thing you have done—you may feel shame. It is almost as if the person is standing in the middle of a circle of people—all of whom are pointing at him or her and saying, "Shame, shame on you. You should be

ashamed of yourself." Shame lowers feelings of self-worth. When you feel ashamed of yourself, your self-esteem gets lower.

SHAME AND OTHER PEOPLE

Shame always involves other people. Sometimes the other people actually see the child doing the wrong thing. Other times, the child just thinks about the other people looking at him or her. In both situations the child is likely to feel shame.

Gloria loved candy. But her mother told her that she was eating too much and warned her that if she didn't stop eating so much candy she'd get fat. Then other children would laugh at her and call her bad names like "fatso" and "fatty." Even though Gloria had not yet gotten fat, these warnings still did not always stop her from eating too much candy.

One day Gloria was shopping with her mother in a supermarket. As they were walking down one of the aisles, Gloria saw lots of candy on the shelves, but she knew her mother wouldn't buy her any. Therefore, while her mother wasn't looking, she took some candy and put it in her pocket.

Later, when the got back into the car, her mother noticed a candy bar sticking out of Gloria's pocket. Her mother looked at her very angrily and said, "You stole that candy from the store. Didn't you, Gloria?" Gloria

was very ashamed of herself and admitted to her mother that she had stolen the candy bar. She took the candy out of her pocket, gave it to her mother and said, "Here, take it back. But don't tell the man that I did it."

Her mother then answered, "No way! You're going to have to face up to what you've done. You're going to have to go into that store and give this candy back to the owner. I know you think I'm being cruel, but you have to learn not to steal. I hope that making you return this candy yourself will help you remember."

Gloria began to cry. She begged her mother not to make her go back into the store and give the candy back to the owner herself: "I'll be very, very embarrassed," she said.

"I'm glad you are," said her mother "but going back will help you remember never to steal again in your whole life."

And so Gloria went back into the store. She told the

owner that she had stolen the candy bar, gave it back to him, and told him how sorry she was for what she had done. The owner took the candy and said, "Thank you for returning my candy. It makes me feel very bad when people steal things from my store. I'm glad that you're being honest about what you did and that you returned it. I can see that you're ashamed and sorry about what you have done. I accept your apology and hope that your embarrassment will help you remember never to steal again."

And that is exactly what happened. Whenever Gloria thought about stealing something, which didn't happen very often, she would think about that day in the store and how ashamed she was of herself for what she had done. And this helped her remember never to steal again. I hope you can see here how shame can be a good thing, even though it can be a very painful feeling.

Another example: Tim stole some baseball cards from his friend's desk in school. His teacher, Mrs. Carlos, saw him do it, gave him a mean look, and said, "Tim, you should be ashamed of yourself. Now you put those cards right back. How would you feel if someone stole your baseball cards?" So Tim put back the baseball cards. At that moment, Tim felt shame. His feelings of self-worth were also lowered because a person important to him had caught him doing something that he knew was wrong.

Later, when Tim would just think about what happened at school, he would feel ashamed of himself. The shameful feelings were not as great as those he had when the teacher actually caught him, but they were still strong enough to make him feel ashamed of himself. His feelings of shame also helped him stop stealing—not only baseball cards, but other things as well.

When he would think about stealing something, he would think about his teacher's disappointment with him and he would become a little ashamed of himself. And that helped him remember not to steal baseball cards or anything else.

An example of this happened two weeks after Tim stole the baseball cards. Tim saw some money on Lucy's desk at school. She had left the money there by mistake. At first, he wanted to steal the money. But,

when he thought about how disappointed Mrs. Carlos would be with him, he felt some shame and so didn't steal the money. He remembered how much shame he suffered when she caught him stealing the baseball cards. Just the picture of her face in his mind caused him enough shame not to steal. It helped him remember not to steal again. He didn't want to suffer the big shame he would have if he were caught stealing again. I hope you can see now how shame always involves other people. Sometimes the other people are actually there, and sometimes you just think about them.

SOMETHING VERY
GOOD ABOUT SHAME

Although shame is a painful feeling to have, it has a good part. It can help people remember not to be bad. Just thinking about how disappointed other people will be can help many children stop doing things that will make them feel ashamed of themselves. Because shame lowers self-esteem, it makes people feel bad about themselves. Therefore, shame helps children remember to be good and so shame can be very useful.

BLUSHING

Blushing is often a part of shame. When people blush, their faces become red and a little puffy. People blush when they are caught doing something wrong. This is especially true when the people who are watching are important to the person who is doing the wrong thing. For example, Carol promised her mother that she would stop taking cookies from the cookie jar when no one was around. She already weighed too much, and her mother wanted her to cut down on sweets and other foods that would make her fat. One day Carol sneaked into the kitchen and started to take some cookies. Just as Carol was about to take the cookie out of the jar, her mother caught her and shouted, "Carol,

you should be ashamed of yourself. You promised me that you wouldn't take cookies without permission. I'm ashamed of you!" At that moment Carol's face became red and puffy. She was blushing. She was ashamed of herself.

People do not blush when they are alone. Although Carol felt shame when she thought about her mother's catching her taking a cookie, she did not blush at that time. You only blush when you're with other people. Blushing is another example of what I said about shame always involving other people. Blushing is one of the ways other people, especially parents, know when a child has done something wrong. It's what parents are talking about when they say to a child, "I can tell you've done something wrong, and I know you're lying. I can tell by that look on your face."

NOT ENOUGH SHAME
AND TOO MUCH SHAME

Not Enough Shame

There are some people who don't have enough shame. Sometimes this happens when parents don't teach children enough about what is good and bad, right and wrong. Such parents never, or hardly ever, say, "You should be ashamed of yourself." Sometimes, the parents themselves don't have very much shame. Because children copy their parents, they don't get ashamed when they do wrong or bad things. Such children get into a lot of trouble. Because they don't have enough shame, they don't use shame to help them remember to be good.

Such children sometimes learn about shame from other people. They may learn about it from teachers and other adults who may tell them that they should be ashamed of themselves when they do bad things. Watching other children being scolded—children who themselves feel ashamed—can sometimes help them learn to have more shame. Such children might learn more about shame if they were to think about all the people who would not like them if they were to learn about or see the bad things they did.

Betsy didn't have enough shame. She would do a lot of bad things, but wasn't ashamed of herself for doing them. One of the bad things she did was to steal from the homes of other children. Because of this everybody said she was a "thief." But this didn't bother her. She wasn't ashamed when they called her a thief. She just kept saying that she wasn't a thief and that the others were lying. As a result, other children stopped inviting her to their homes. Betsy then became

68

a sad and lonely person. If she had learned to feel shame she might have stopped stealing and then she probably would have had many friends.

Too Much Shame

There are some children who are just the opposite. They have too much shame. They get ashamed very easily. Sometimes these children have parents who have said too often, "You should be ashamed of yourself." After every little bad or wrong thing they did their parents were always saying things like, "Shame, shame on you. You're making us ashamed of you. You should be ashamed of yourself." Some of these children have parents who have too much shame themselves. Because children copy their parents, they easily become ashamed as well. They blush very easily. They may become very shy and are afraid to do many things that other children do because they are always afraid they'll do the wrong thing.

Such children can help themselves with their shame problem by remembering that no one is perfect, and that everyone does wrong or bad things once in a while. If they keep reminding themselves of this, they will often not feel ashamed every time they do some little, wrong thing.

PAIN, PLEASURE, AND SHAME

In the last chapter, Chapter Two, I spoke about how little babies learn mainly from pain and pleasure. They are too young to remember things for very long. Therefore, the best way for little babies to learn what is good and bad, right and wrong, is to connect good things with pleasure and bad things with pain. Little babies are too young to think about shame and feel ashamed of themselves.

As children grow older, they become able to feel shame and think shameful thoughts. This is a good thing because it helps them avoid doing bad things. Therefore, it helps keep children from being punished. It is an additional way of helping children remember to be good and do good things. Older children can also learn from pleasure and pain, and this too helps them remember not to do bad things.

You have to be older than an infant to feel shame. You have to have a better memory than a little baby to feel shame. And you have to be able to understand better than a little baby the difference between right and wrong in order to feel shame. Once people are old enough to feel shame, they can feel shame at any time in life—no matter how long they live. However, most people do fewer shameful things as they grow older because they have learned from their experiences with shame. They have learned that it is better **not** to do the wrong thing than to suffer the shame of being caught doing it. They have learned that just the thought of important people being disappointed with them can make them ashamed enough not to do the bad thing. In this way they protect themselves from feelings of low self-worth. In this way they may enjoy feelings of high self-esteem.

IMPORTANT THINGS
TO REMEMBER

1. Shame is the kind of feeling of low self-worth that comes when people who are important to you discover that you have done something bad or wrong.

2. Shame always involves other people.

3. Shameful thoughts come into your mind when you think about other people being disappointed with you when they see you doing the wrong thing.

4. Shameful feelings also come when other people actually see you doing the wrong thing. Then you feel ashamed of yourself.

5. Shame is useful. Shame helps people remember not to do bad things. Remembering how ashamed a person was when caught doing a bad thing can help that person not do the bad thing again.

6. Too little shame is bad because the person then gets into a lot of trouble.

7. Too much shame is bad because it lowers self-esteem more than is necessary.

8. I hope that you have just the right amount of shame.

Guilt

WHAT IS GUILT?

Guilt is another kind of feeling of low self-worth. People may feel guilt after **doing** things that they have learned are bad or wrong to do. People may also feel guilt after having **feelings** that they have learned are bad or wrong to feel. And people may feel guilt after thinking **thoughts** that they have learned are bad or wrong to think. I hope you have noticed the word **may** here. I will talk more about the word **may** later.

THE DIFFERENCE BETWEEN SHAME AND GUILT

There is a big difference between shame and guilt. As I said in Chapter Three, shame always involves other people. Sometimes the other people are not actually there, and sometimes they are. When they are not there you imagine that important people are telling you how disappointed they are because of what you have said or done. Or you may be ashamed because you actually have been seen doing or saying the bad things. In these ways shame lowers feelings of self-worth.

When you have guilt, the disappointed person is not any of these other people. When you have guilt the disappointed person is **you yourself**. You feel bad about yourself for what you have thought, felt, or done. Therefore, you can feel guilt when you are all alone. Even at night, when you are all alone in your room, when there is no one around to see you, you can feel guilt. Even when you hide under the covers, you can feel guilt. In this way guilt lowers feelings of self-worth.

PLEASURE AND PAIN,
SHAME AND GUILT

In Chapter Two I spoke about how very young children only learn from pleasure and pain. In Chapter Three I spoke about how children, as they get older, can understand more and remember better. Such children can then use shame to help them remember not to do bad things. In order to feel guilt the child has to be even older. To have guilt you have to be able to understand even more and you have to be able to remember even better.

To feel guilt you must be able to feel bad about things you have done that have hurt other people. Little babies can't do this. And even younger children—children who can feel shame—may still not be able to feel bad about hurting other people. Such children, therefore, can't feel guilt. In the next chapter, Chapter Five, I will say more about feeling bad when you have hurt other people's feelings.

There is another big difference between guilt and the other ways of helping people remember to be good. The difference has to do with whether or not people must be around. For a baby to learn from pleasure and pain there must be people around to watch the baby and give it love when it is good and to take away love, or to punish, when it is bad. For shame to work other people also must be involved. Sometimes they are actually there at the time when the child does the bad thing. Then they tell the child how disappointed they are about what the child has done. Sometimes the child's just thinking about being seen by important people causes enough shameful feelings to help the child remember not to do the bad thing. When children use guilt to help them stop doing wrong things, other people do not have to be around to watch. Other people can do other things.

Most grownups like guilt better than shame, or pleasure and pain. Most adults believe that guilt is the best way for a child to remember to be good. When children are old enough to feel guilt, adults don't have to spend so much time watching the children and reminding them to be good. The adults can then do other things instead, things that may be much more interesting and fun than just acting like a guard or watchdog for a child.

Guilt is a very good way to help someone remember not to do bad or wrong things. For example, Alice's friend Carla lost five dollars. Alice found the money in her own house. The money had dropped out of Carla's pocket when she was playing at Alice's house. At first, Alice thought of keeping the money.

She knew she could get away with keeping it because Carla had no way of knowing that she had lost the money at Alice's house. But Alice knew that stealing was bad. She knew that the person whose money was stolen feels bad and angry. She knew that she would feel bad about herself—even when she was all alone—if she stole the money. After she thought about it, she decided not to keep the money, but to give it to Carla. When she did this, Carla said, "Thank you Alice. You're a very honest person. You could have kept the money and I would never have known it. Some people would have done that. You're a very good friend." Alice then felt very good about herself. Her self-esteem went up very high. Had she kept the money she would have felt guilty and her self-esteem would have been very low. She felt the good feelings of high self-worth that come from being honest. Therefore, avoiding guilt

protects us from feeling low self-worth. And then doing the good thing instead gives us feelings of high self-worth.

NOT ENOUGH GUILT
OR TOO MUCH GUILT

There are two very big problems with guilt. The first is that there are many people who don't have enough guilt. The second is that there are some people who have too much guilt. Both are problems. It is best to have just the right amount of guilt, not too little, and not too much. Now I will discuss each of these two kinds of problems and tell you what you can do about each one if you have either one of them.

Not Enough Guilt

There are some people who do not have enough guilt. There are many reasons why a person could grow up and not have enough guilt. Probably the most common reason is that the child's parents haven't taught the child about good and bad, about right and wrong. The parents may not have helped the child learn about other people's feelings, and how bad others feel when someone does bad things to them. Sometimes the parents themselves have too little guilt. Because children copy their parents, the children too grow up without having enough guilt. Sometimes a child will have parents who have taught the child about guilt, but the child made the wrong kinds of friends— friends who didn't have enough guilt themselves and who did bad things.

People who don't have enough guilt may get into a lot of trouble. In school they may get into trouble with their teachers and their friends. They do just what they want, when they want to. They make so much trouble in the classroom that other children can't learn. Often, the teacher may have to send them out of the classroom—even to the principal's office—so that others can learn. Worse than the punishment these children get is their not learning very much in school. And this is a very bad thing to happen. Then, they don't know the answers to the teacher's questions and get embarrassed in the classroom. And if they continue not learning very much in school they grow up not knowing very much. And this can cause a person a lot of trouble throughout life.

When such children grow older and become teenagers, they may turn into what are often called "juvenile delinquents." They may lie, steal, and cause a lot

of trouble for other people. Sometimes juvenile delinquents even get into trouble with the police. Because

juvenile delinquents do not have enough guilt, they do not feel bad when they do the wrong things, and so they get into a lot of trouble. They do not get bad feelings inside themselves when they think about doing the wrong thing. And so they do not get the kinds of feelings that can help them remember to be good. Because of this, some of them even grow up to become criminals and go to jail. Most juvenile delinquents, however, do learn some guilt as they grow older and so they do not end up in jail.

Too Much Guilt

The second kind of problem with guilt is that some people have too much of it. Such people suffer with low self-worth after doing anything wrong at all, no matter how small. All children—even those who are very, very good—do bad things once in a while. This is how children learn right from wrong. After doing a bad thing and getting punished or feeling shame, or feeling guilt, the child is less likely to do the bad thing again. But everybody makes mistakes, at times. Everybody forgets at times and does the wrong thing. No one in the whole, wide world is perfect. Children with too much guilt don't seem to know this. Even when they make a little mistake their self-esteem gets very low for a long time. They keep thinking over and over again how terrible they are. These children just can't forget about the small mistakes they make and the bad things they do once in a while. These children have too much guilt.

Sometimes such children have had parents who have made them feel very guilty over even the smallest wrong things. Their parents have often said such things as: "How can you do such terrible things?"

"What a terrible thing to say." "You shouldn't even **think** such things." Some children with too much guilt have parents who also have too much guilt and who are very strict with themselves. They think that everyone should be perfect and never, or hardly ever, do anything wrong. Because children copy their parents, the children become the same way.

Children with too much guilt may think that it's always terrible to do anything bad. They think it's terrible to be bad, even once. They don't seem to understand that it's **normal** to be bad once in a while. Such children suffer with very low feelings of self-worth. If they could change their minds and realize that no one is perfect, that everyone does bad things once in a while, they would feel less guilty. They would then feel better about themselves.

Children who have too much guilt have to learn that thoughts and feelings are **not** the same as acts. What you think and feel are not the same as what you do. Unfortunately, there are parents who say to their children, "What a terrible child you are for saying such a thing! You shouldn't even **think** such thoughts." This is a very cruel thing for a parent to say to a child. We have no control at all over our thoughts. They just pop into our minds whenever they want to. And this is also true about our feelings. They often just come over us. We most often have no control over them. We do, however, have control over our **acts**, that is, what we **do**. These we **can** control. These we can stop.

For example, Stan thought it would be a lot of fun to throw a rock through a window. However, when he thought about the feelings of the people whose window would be broken he decided not to throw the rock. When he thought about this he felt guilty and he threw the rock on the ground. This is a good example of how

we can control our acts. It is also an example of how guilt can help us stop doing bad things.

Another example: Doris was very angry at her mother. Doris' mother said she had to turn off the television and go to bed because it was late and she had to get up very early the next day to go to school. Doris was very angry. She got so upset that she called her mother some bad names and used some dirty words. Her mother said: "I can understand your thinking

those thoughts, but it's wrong to say such things to me. I can understand that you're angry that I made you turn off the television set. I can understand your feeling like calling me bad names. But it's just not permitted. When you're angry at me you'll have to use words that are more polite."

Doris' mother was a very smart woman. She did not make Doris feel guilty about her angry thoughts and feelings. She tried, however, to make her feel guilty about what she **did** which was to use dirty words to her mother. The next time Doris' mother did something Doris didn't like, Doris had the same angry thoughts and the same angry feelings, but she didn't feel guilty about them. Also, she told her mother how angry she was—but used words that were more polite than those that popped into her mind. So then she didn't feel guilty and her self-esteem remained high.

There is no thought—no matter how terrible—that doesn't come into everyone's mind at some time. There is nothing wrong or bad about having such thoughts. And there is no feeling—no matter how terrible—that isn't felt by everyone at some time. There is nothing bad or wrong about having such feelings. It is only **doing** bad things that are wrong. Doing the bad thing gets you into trouble and should make you feel guilty. Most bad thoughts and feelings are normal and are okay to have as long as you don't do bad things when you have them. If you are the kind of a person who has too much guilt, then you should think a lot about what I have just said here. If you do, then you will feel less guilty about your thoughts and feelings.

Just the Right Amount of Guilt

The best thing, then, is to have just the right amount of guilt—not too little, and not too much. People with too little guilt often get into a lot of trouble with other people because of the many bad things they do. People with too much guilt often suffer with feelings of low self-esteem. People who are in the middle know that it's okay to do bad things once in a while, but most of the time they are good and try not to hurt other people's feelings. These people are in the middle and have the highest feelings of self-worth. They are the people who feel best about themselves.

NORMAL AND HEALTHY WAYS OF MAKING GUILT GO AWAY

Because everyone does bad or wrong things, at least once in a while, everyone feels guilt, at least once in a while.

Saying You're Sorry

One way of lowering guilt is to say you're sorry, that is, to apologize. However, it is very important to remember that there are two different ways of saying you're sorry. One way is to say you're sorry when you really don't mean it, and the other way is to say you're sorry when you really mean it.

Saying You're Sorry When You Don't Mean It
Many people just say they're sorry when they don't mean it in order to stay out of trouble. They say it so that the other person will forgive them. Often the other person doesn't forgive them, but doesn't say anything about it. People who do this don't really get away with it. The other person is still angry and will often have nothing to do with people who say they're sorry when they really don't mean it. I hope you aren't the kind of person who says "I'm sorry" and doesn't really mean it, who lies that way to stay out of trouble.

Johnny was that kind of person. He used to hit his sister a lot and his mother kept telling him to say he was sorry. Johnny would then say he was sorry, but he

really didn't mean it. He just said he was sorry so his mother wouldn't punish him. His sister knew that he was lying and so she still remained angry. She wouldn't forgive him. Later, she wouldn't play with him because she was still angry. She wouldn't play with him because she knew he was lying when he said he was sorry. And she wouldn't forgive him for the rest of the day. Also, Johnny's guilt did not go away. He knew that he had done a bad thing. And his sister's not forgiving him caused him to still have the guilt.

Saying You're Sorry When You Really Mean It
There are many people, however, who only say they're sorry when they really mean it. They realize that they have hurt the other person's feelings and really want to be forgiven for what they have done wrong. Such people really feel guilty about what they have done. And, when such people say they're sorry, the other person believes them and usually forgives them. Then, they no longer feel any guilt.

And this is what happened with Martha. While she was playing at her friend Edith's house, she got very angry and jumped on one of Edith's dolls. After Martha did that Edith began to cry. Martha then also got very upset and felt guilty about what she had done. She then apologized to Edith and told her that she was sorry. She also told her that she would give her one of her own dolls. She was really sorry that she had lost her temper. She felt very guilty about what she had done. Edith told Martha that she would accept her apology because she knew Martha really meant it when she said she was sorry. Edith also told Martha that it wasn't necessary to give her a doll because the doll was an old one anyway.

Getting Punishment

Often punishment can stop guilt. A person has done something wrong, gets punished for it, and then no longer has to feel guilty about what was done. This is certainly the way it works for grownups who commit crimes. A man steals a lot of money and the judge tells him that he is going to go to jail. While in jail the man is being punished for the crime he committed. After he gets out, he no longer has to feel guilty. He has been punished for his crime. The same thing is true for children who are bad. For example, Johnny spilled his milk on his baby sister's head. He did it on purpose. It wasn't an accident. He thought that was a fun thing to do. Johnny's parents were very upset with him. They

both yelled at him. While they were doing this he felt very guilty about what he had done. They told him that he would have to spend one hour alone in his room, standing in the corner. This was the punishment for the bad thing he had done. This punishment stopped his guilt. When he got out of the room he no longer felt guilty.

Punishment not only makes guilt go away but it can also help a person remember not to do the wrong thing again. Therefore, it is like the pain that little babies feel, the pain which helps them remember not to do bad things.

Of course, the fewer bad things you do, the less guilt you will feel, and the less punishment you will need to lessen your guilt.

Confessing

Confession means telling some important person that you have done the wrong thing and asking the person to forgive you for it. Sometimes, a person will do a wrong thing and keep it a big secret. Such people are ashamed to tell anyone and are afraid that everyone will hate them for what has been done. They may go around for weeks or even months, never telling anyone about the wrong thing that was done. They may even think that there will be terrible punishments that will follow. Confessing what was done, and asking the other person to forgive, can often help reduce guilt. The person may then learn that the punishment that was expected may not be great at all, or may not even happen.

This is what happened with Linda. Her grandmother had given her a ten-dollar bill as a birthday present. Her mother told her to put it in her drawer so she wouldn't lose it. Linda didn't listen to her mother. Instead, she took it to school in order to show her friends. However, she lost it on the way to school. It fell out of her pocket while she was walking. When Linda got to school she realized that she had lost the money. She was very upset. She felt very guilty about not having listened to her mother. She also felt very bad about the money that she had lost. She had done the wrong thing; she hadn't listened to her mother.

For the next week Linda was afraid to tell her mother. She was sure that her mother would give her a very big punishment. Her mother noticed how sad and gloomy Linda looked. During that time, whenever her mother asked her what was wrong, Linda said, "Oh, nothing. Nothing's wrong!" Her mother told her that

she didn't believe her, but Linda still kept saying that nothing was wrong.

Finally, at the end of the week, her mother once again asked her if something was wrong. At that point Linda could hold it in no longer. She began crying and told her mother that she had lost the ten dollars. Linda was surprised when her mother said: "I'm not going to punish you. You've already received your punishment. Your punishment was losing the ten dollars. Had you listened to me you wouldn't have lost the ten dollars. That's enough punishment. Also, you punished yourself even more by walking around for a whole week and not telling me. Your guilty feelings were your second punishment. And that punishment was not necessary. No matter when you had told me about the ten dollars, I wouldn't have done any terrible thing to you."

After that Linda felt much better. She had confessed to her mother what had happened. Her mother had forgiven her and didn't punish her. Then all her guilt went away.

Now it doesn't always happen that when you confess you will get no punishment. Sometimes people who confess still get punishments, but they usually get smaller punishments than those they would get if they didn't confess. This is what happens to grownups when they commit a crime and go to court. If they confess and admit that they committed the crime, they will often get less of a punishment than if they lied and said they didn't commit the crime when they really did. The reason for this is that if they confess the judge can make a quick decision about what punishment to give the person. However, when people lie and say they didn't commit a crime that they really did, then the judge and the jury have to go to a lot of trouble to try to find out what really happened. Because of this extra trouble the person may get a bigger punishment.

And something like this happened to Ralph. One day Ralph and his brother Peter were playing in their room. Ralph showed Peter a package of matches that he had found. Ralph then started lighting the matches, one at a time, and then throwing them up in the air. He thought that was a lot of fun. Peter got scared and told Ralph that he was doing a dangerous thing and that something might catch on fire. Ralph laughed at Peter and said that nothing like that would happen and that the matches always burned out when you threw them in the air. Their mother was downstairs and didn't know what was going on. However, as Ralph was doing this, they suddenly heard their mother coming up the stairs. At that point Ralph threw the package of matches behind his bed.

When their mother came into the room, she smelled the smoke immediately and saw the burned matches on the floor. She became very upset and asked the boys who was playing with matches. Ralph immediately pointed to Peter and said, "Peter did it!"

Peter immediately replied, "Mom, he's lying."

Ralph then said, "No Mom, he's the liar. He's a big, fat liar. I saw him do it."

Peter then began crying and said, "He's the liar. He's the one who played with the matches. And he just took them and threw them behind his bed."

Their mother then said: "Fire-setting is a crime. It's a crime because it's a very dangerous thing to do. People can be burned to death. This whole house could have burned down and we might have all died. However, it's going to be very easy to solve this crime."

She then walked over to the bed, took out a handkerchief, and with it picked up the package of matches. She then said, "This package of matches has the fingerprints of the person who was using them. It's going to be very easy for me to solve this crime. All I have to do is take you both down to the police station and have you both fingerprinted. Then I can ask the police to see whose fingerprints are on this package of matches. I'm holding the matchbook with a handkerchief so I won't ruin or smear the fingerprints."

Then Peter cried out, "That's a great idea. Let's go down right now. The police will prove that I'm telling the truth and that Ralph's the big, fat liar!"

At that point the mother turned to Ralph and said, "Ralph, what do you think about that?"

Ralph was silent. He just sat there saying nothing.

He was trying to think of a good reason for not going down to the police station. He knew that if he went down there that the police would prove that he was the

one who lit the matches. He didn't know what to say. He couldn't think of a good reason for not going to the police. Then, before he knew what was happening, he suddenly burst into tears and said, "Okay, I did it. I'm sorry I did it. I didn't think it was so dangerous. Please don't punish me."

Ralph's mother said: "Ralph, you did two bad things. First, you did a very dangerous thing by playing with matches. For that you will get the first punishment. Second, you lied about it and tried to put the blame on your brother. That was the second bad thing, and for that you're going to get a second punishment.

The first punishment is no television for two weeks, even your favorite television programs. I hope that will help you remember not to play with matches ever again. And the second punishment is no allowance for two weeks. I hope that punishment will help you remember never to lie again. If you had admitted at the beginning that you were the one who played with the matches, I would have given you only one punishment. But since you did two bad things, you're getting two punishments."

When the two weeks were over Ralph no longer had to feel guilty about what he had done. He had confessed, said he was sorry, and gotten punished. He realized how dangerous fire-setting was and how bad lying was. He never set fires again and never blamed his brother for something that he had done.

There are some parents who will say to a child, "Confess that you did it and I won't punish you." In my opinion this is a big mistake. A judge would never say to a person in court, "Confess you committed the crime, and I won't punish you." A judge might say: "If you confess now, and save the court a lot of time and trouble, I'll give you a small punishment. However, if you lie, and make me go to a lot of trouble to find out whether you did it, I'll give you a bigger punishment." In the same way, what a parent should say is this: "If you confess, I'll just punish you for the wrong thing you did. However, if you lie about it, and then I later find out that you did it, you'll get a **double** punishment. You'll get one punishment for the wrong thing you did, and the second punishment for lying." That's what Ralph's mother did, and that's what all parents should do.

Again, the fewer bad things you do, the less guilt you will feel, and the less confessing you will need to do to lessen your guilt.

Compensation

There is another way of helping yourself feel less guilty. That other way is called **compensation**. Compensation means giving something to the person you have hurt or harmed in order to make up for their pain or loss. When you do this we say that you have compensated the person for the harm that was done. After that, the other person may not feel any pain, loss, or anger and the person who gave compensation need no longer feel guilt.

Jeffrey liked building models. He did this very well and was very proud of the things he made. One of the models he was proudest of was of a boat. Everyone said that he had done a "beautiful job" and his father put it over the fireplace so everyone could see it when they came into the house. One day, while Jeffrey was at a friend's house, his two brothers, Gary and Stanley, were rough-housing in the living room. Their mother told them not to play in the house, but to go outside. However, the two boys didn't listen to her and they continued to horse around in the house. They began to jump up and down, making believe they were horses. While they were playing "horsie," Jeffrey's boat fell off the shelf over the fireplace. They were making so much noise that they didn't hear the boat fall off the shelf. They just continued hopping around the room and suddenly, without realizing what they were doing, they jumped on Jeffrey's boat—which had landed on the floor in front of the fireplace.

As soon as they realized what they had done, both boys became very frightened. They knew that when Jeffrey came home he would be very upset and that he would probably cry. They knew how much the boat meant to Jeffrey and how proud he was about having

CRUNCH!

101

built it. They also felt very guilty about what they had done.

When their mother found out about the boat she screamed at Gary and Stanley, and this made them feel even more guilty. After talking about what had happened with their mother, they decided that the best thing to do would be to give Jeffrey enough money to buy **two** boats. He could use half the money to buy another model boat and the other half to buy yet another model. In this way Jeffrey would not feel so bad about his boat being smashed. They hoped that with this **compensation** Jeffrey would not be so sad and angry and that the two brothers, then, would not have to feel so much guilt.

And this is exactly what happened. When Jeffrey came home, and learned that his brothers had smashed his boat, he began to cry. He was very sad and angry at the same time. His brothers then told him that they had talked to their mother about it and all agreed that they would save up from their allowances and give him double the cost of the boat. When Jeffrey realized that he would now have enough money to buy **two** boats, he stopped crying and he didn't feel so sad and angry. And his brothers then didn't feel any more guilt. Giving Jeffrey compensation caused their guilt to go away.

Once again, the fewer bad things you do, the less guilt you will feel, and the less compensation you will need to do in order to lessen your guilt.

Saying you're sorry when you really mean it, accepting punishment, confessing, and giving compensation are four important ways of making guilt go away. But the best thing, of course, is not to do the bad thing in the first place. Then you will have nothing to feel guilty about. Then there will be nothing to apologize for, there will be no punishments, there will be nothing to confess, and there will be nothing for which you will have to provide compensation.

IMPORTANT THINGS
TO REMEMBER

1. Guilt is a kind of feeling of low self-worth that comes after thinking thoughts, feeling feelings, or doing things that are bad or wrong.

2. Guilt helps people remember not to do bad things. It does this by causing them to feel bad about themselves if they do bad things.

3. People with not enough guilt get into a lot of trouble. It can ruin their whole lives.

4. People with too much guilt can suffer with many feelings of low self-esteem that are not necessary.

5. The best thing is something in the middle, not too much guilt and not too little guilt.

6. Saying you're sorry when you really mean it can help lower guilt.

7. Accepting punishment for what you have done can also lower guilt.

8. Confessing what you have done can also lower guilt.

9. Compensating the person harmed by the wrong thing you have done can also lower guilt.

10. The best thing, however, is not to do bad or wrong things. Then there will be no guilt.

11. However no one is perfect. Everyone does wrong or bad things once in a while, and so most people feel some guilt once in a while.

CHAPTER 5

Sympathy

WHAT IS SYMPATHY?

When I use the word **sympathy**, I am talking about the ability to feel the same feelings that another person feels. When a person has sympathy we say that he or she is sympathetic. For example, Nancy and Julie were very good friends. One day Nancy's father told them that he was going to take both of them to the circus on Saturday. They were both very excited thinking about all the fun they would have at the circus. They kept counting the days to Saturday. However, early Saturday morning Julie got sick and could not go to the circus. But Nancy and her father still went. This made Julie very sad. And even while she was at the circus Nancy felt sad too when she thought about her friend

Julie. Here Nancy had the same feelings as Julie. We say that Nancy was sympathetic.

Sympathy is very important to have. If you have little or no sympathy you will usually get into a lot of trouble with other people.

PUTTING YOURSELF IN ANOTHER PERSON'S SHOES

Sometimes people will say, "Put yourself in the other person's shoes." When people say that they are not really thinking that you should actually wear the other person's shoes. What they mean is that you should try to **think about** what the other person might be feeling. They are asking you to try to **feel** the same way the other person might be feeling.

106

Myra and Jack had a good chance to learn how to do this. Their mother was a very good cook. Both of them loved her apple pie. One day, they both asked her for some pie and she told them that she had only one piece left. Each child began pleading for that piece of pie. The mother then suggested that they cut the pie in half and each take one piece.

Myra then said, "Mommy, give me the bread knife, I'll cut the pie in two."

Jack replied, "No. I don't trust her. She'll cut herself the bigger piece."

Myra said, "No I won't. You can trust me. I'll make the two pieces equal."

Jack then said, "I don't trust you. Last time you did that you cut yourself the bigger piece."

Finally their mother said, "I have a good idea. One of you will cut the pie, and the other one will

choose first! Therefore, if you do not cut evenly, you will end up with the smaller piece."

The children both thought that was a good idea. So Myra very carefully cut the pie and tried as hard as she could to make the parts equal. She did it so well that Jack had a hard time trying to figure out which was the larger piece. Both children learned something useful that day. They both learned something about putting yourself in another person's shoes.

Another example of sympathy: Roger stole a computer toy from his friend Mark. Although he hid it in his room when he got home, his mother found it and asked him where he got the toy. She knew that neither she nor Roger's father had bought the toy for him. Roger was ashamed of himself and admitted to his mother that he had stolen the toy from Mark.

His mother then said, "You should be ashamed of yourself, stealing your friend's toy. Think about how you'd feel if someone stole your computer toy. Put yourself in his shoes." When Roger heard what his mother said he felt even worse. He hadn't thought before about how Mark would feel after he learned that his toy was missing. He felt ashamed in front of his mother about what he had done. He felt guilty inside himself for having stolen the toy. He felt sad himself when he realized how sad Mark would be when he learned that the toy was stolen. So he brought the toy back to Mark and confessed to him that he had stolen the toy and said that he meant it when he said he was sorry. Roger promised him that he would never do that again. Mark could see that Roger wasn't lying and that he really was sorry. So Mark forgave Roger. He said that he would still be his friend. Then Roger no longer

felt ashamed or guilty. And neither of them then felt sad because Mark got his toy back and Roger didn't have anything else to feel sympathetic about. Also, Roger never stole again because he had learned how bad people feel when something is stolen from them. He had learned to be sympathetic. The feelings of sympathy helped him remember to be good. And that is one of the important things about sympathy; it helps people remember to treat other people well.

THE GOLDEN RULE

There is an old saying, called **The Golden Rule**. Although it can be found in the Bible, it is probably even older than that. The saying is: "Do unto others as you would have others do unto you." Some of you may not know exactly what that means because some of the words are like those used in olden times. The saying means that you should treat other people in the exact same way you would want other people to treat you.

We all want other people to be nice to us. The best way to make this happen is to be nice to other people. If everybody treated everyone else the same way we wanted to be treated by others, then we would all be nicer to one another and it would be a better world.

This is such an important idea that it has been called a **rule** so that people will remember to follow it. A rule is an idea that people are supposed to follow. This rule is called the Golden Rule because it is so valuable and precious that it is like gold.

The Golden Rule has a lot to do with sympathy. In order to treat other people as you would like to be treated by them, you have to have sympathy for other people. You have to be able to put yourself in the other person's shoes, as the saying goes. If all people were to be sympathetic to one another, all would be following the Golden Rule. We would then all be nicer to one another and it would be a much better world.

SYMPATHY AND SELF-ESTEEM

Your self-esteem gets higher when you do things that everyone agrees are good things to do. Most people agree that being sympathetic is a good thing. Therefore, when you are sympathetic you feel good about yourself. This is especially true when you give up something of your own in order to be sympathetic.

For example, a woman came to Paul's class and spoke about sick children in the hospital who wouldn't be home for Christmas. Some of these sick children were also very poor, and so would not be getting

Christmas presents. And some were so sick that they were going to die soon and would never have another Christmas. She asked the children to help by giving toys.

Paul felt bad about the sick children in the hospital—especially those who were going to die soon. He

was a very sympathetic person. So he gave some of his best toys. It was not easy for him to do this; in fact it hurt. However, after he gave the toys, he felt very good about himself for doing such a kind thing. His feelings of self-esteem therefore got higher. Being sympathetic, then, can raise self-worth. Also, it often makes another person feel better as well.

112

SYMPATHY, PLEASURE, AND PAIN

Little babies cannot be sympathetic. They just don't understand enough. They can't put themselves in another person's place. For example, this baby was sucking milk from its mother's breast. While sucking the breast, the baby bit the mother's nipple. This hurt the

mother very much and she screamed out. But she knew that the baby didn't understand and so she didn't punish the baby.

She might have been able to teach the baby to stop biting her by hitting the baby each time it bit her. If she did this many times—each time right after the baby bit her—the baby might have learned to stop biting. It

113

would not have learned from any real understanding. It only would have learned that each time it bit the mother's nipple it would suffer pain. And the baby certainly would not have learned sympathy. The baby could not understand or feel the mother's pain. Also, to teach the baby by hitting it each time it bit the mother's nipple would have been a cruel thing to do. Such a mother has little if any sympathy for her baby. Most mothers know that a baby will not bite her breast very often and so do nothing special about the baby's biting them once in a while. If it happens often, then they can do something else, like feed the baby from a bottle.

The main thing I want to say here is that babies are not old enough to have sympathy. They do not understand how other people feel, and they cannot, therefore, feel sympathy.

SYMPATHY AND SHAME

As a baby grows older it can learn to be sympathetic. By the time the child is old enough to understand enough to be ashamed it can also **start** to understand a little about sympathy. Some of the things a child might be ashamed about involve hurting other people or even animals. That's where sympathy comes in. At that young age a child can be taught to be kind to pets. It can learn that being cruel to an animal hurts the animal.

Most often, Dan was very kind to his dog, Floppy. However, when Dan would get upset about something he could be very cruel to Floppy. For example, one day Dan had been very bad and so his mother punished him by sending him to his room for a half-hour. When he got into his room, Floppy was there. The first thing Dan did was to kick Floppy. Floppy screeched out so

loud that Dan's mother heard the dog downstairs. She ran up to the room and saw Floppy hiding under the bed. The dog was trying to protect itself from Dan. She asked Dan what had happened. At first Dan said, "Nothing." His mother told him that she knew Dan was lying and that he'd better tell the truth or he wouldn't be allowed to watch television for one week. So Dan told her the truth. He told her that he was angry about being sent to his room and so he kicked Floppy.

His mother then said: "That was a very cruel thing to do to your dog. You should know better. You should be ashamed of yourself. Have you no feelings for that dog? Have you no sympathy? For kicking the dog you have to stay in your room an extra half-hour, and for lying about it still another half-hour. I hope that will help you remember to be more sympathetic to your dog."

Dan was ashamed of himself. The punishment helped him remember not to kick the dog again. Also, the shame he felt over what he had done also helped him remember to be more sympathetic and not to be cruel.

SYMPATHY AND GUILT

By the time children are old enough to feel guilt they should be able to feel even more sympathy than younger children. Guilt and sympathy go together. As I said in Chapter Four, to feel guilt it is often important to understand how another person feels, especially someone you have harmed or hurt.

Helen was playing at her girlfriend Ruth's house. Ruth's mother had told them not to run around the house and if they wanted to run they should do so in the back yard. But the two girls didn't listen. As they were running through the living room, Ruth knocked down a vase and it smashed all over the floor. Ruth's

mother came into the room and asked who knocked down the vase. Each girl pointed to the other one. Ruth's mother said that it must have been Helen because her daughter would never lie to her. And so Ruth's mother sent Helen home. Helen was very angry as she left the house. Not only was she angry, but she was crying. As she left the house she screamed back at Ruth, "Ruth, you're a big, fat liar!" Then she slammed the door. You might think that Ruth would feel guilty for having lied and blamed Helen for having broken the vase that she herself had knocked over. But instead she was glad that she had gotten away with it. She wasn't sympathetic to how Helen felt. She didn't feel guilty. Guilt and sympathy often go together. If you don't have sympathy you may not have guilt.

After that Helen would no longer be friends with Ruth. At school, she wouldn't even talk to her. When

Helen saw Ruth coming down the hall she just stared straight ahead as if Ruth didn't exist. She walked with her nose in the air and made believe that she didn't know that Ruth was there. This made Ruth feel very lonely and sad. Ruth knew why Helen was angry at her. Because of her lying Ruth had lost a friend. This is a good example of what can happen to people who don't have sympathy. Nice people don't want to have anything to do with them. People who don't have sympathy, or who have very little, have trouble making friends. Or, if they do make them, they lose them because no one wants to be friends with a person who doesn't care about other people's feelings.

SYMPATHY AND SHARING

Most children don't like to share. But sharing and sympathy go together. Unfortunately, there are some

118

children who hardly ever share at all. They aren't considerate of other people's feelings. When a friend comes to their home, they don't want to share their toys and always want to go first. They don't think about the feelings of their guests. They don't have sympathy for their guests. They don't feel guilty about how badly they treat their guests. Such children end up very lonely, because no one wants to come to their homes again. I hope you're not this kind of child.

SOME IMPORTANT THINGS
TO REMEMBER

1. Sympathy is the ability to think about another person's feelings and to feel the same feelings the other person feels.

2. The Golden Rule is a good example of sympathy. The Golden Rule says: "Do unto others as you would have others do unto you." This means that you should treat others in the same way you would like others to treat you.

3. If you don't have sympathy you may not be ashamed of the bad things you do to other people. Therefore, other people will not want to be with you, and you'll be very lonely.

4. If you don't have sympathy you may not feel guilty about the bad things you do to other people. And so other people will not want to be with you and you'll be very lonely.

CHAPTER 6

Stop, Look, Listen, and Think

THE PAST, PRESENT, AND FUTURE

The past, present, and future all have something to do with time. They also have something to do with good and bad behavior, and that is why I will be talking about them here.

The Present Time

The present time is what is happening right now. What you are now reading is being read in the present. You are reading this book at the present time.

The Past Time

The past is all the things that have ever happened before the present. One second ago, one minute ago,

121

and one hour ago are all part of the past. But the past goes even further back. One day ago, one year ago, one hundred years ago, and as far back as the beginning of the world are all in the past.

The Future Time

The future refers to all the things that will happen after the present. The future could be one second from now, one hour from now, or one day from now. It could also be much further ahead in time, such as one year from now or a hundred years from now. It might even go on forever.

THE PAST AND MEMORY

It is important to remember certain things that happened in the past, especially mistakes. People who don't remember their mistakes may make them again and get into lots of trouble. Pain, shame, and guilt help us remember our past mistakes. They help us remember not to make the same mistakes again. That's why pain, shame, and guilt can be so useful. Remembering how we felt in the past can help us stop doing those things which caused us pain, shame, and guilt in the past. Remembering how we may have hurt or harmed people in the past can help us become more sympathetic.

THINKING ABOUT THE
PRESENT AND CONCENTRATION

We can remember the past, but we think about the present. The more we think about the present, the more we can do about problems that we may be having in the present. To do this, a person has to slow down and think carefully. This is called **concentration**. When people are concentrating they are usually thinking slowly and carefully about the present. I will say much more later about concentration.

THINKING ABOUT THE FUTURE AND PREDICTIONS

A prediction is a guess about what is going to happen in the future. For example, a person might say, "I predict that it will snow so heavily tomorrow that school will be closed." That's called a prediction. Sometimes predic-

tions turn out to be true and sometimes they do not. Some predictions are very good ones, and some very bad. For example, if a boy does not do any homework, it's easy to predict that he will get a very low grade. That is an example of a good prediction because it usually turns out to be true. A bad prediction is that a girl who does no homework will get very high grades in all her subjects on her report card. That is an example of a prediction that is not true. That's a bad prediction.

IMPULSIVITY AND CONSEQUENCES

Doing something without thinking carefully about what is going to happen in the future is called **impulsivity.** The person acts without concentrating, without thinking carefully about what he or she is doing. Impulsivity happens in the present. People who are impulsive are not thinking about the future. We call people impulsive when they do things without thinking carefully about what they are doing and what will happen in the future as the result of their acts.

Consequences are the things that happen after we have done something. Consequences take place in the future. When people are impulsive they usually don't think at that time about future consequences. They don't concentrate and they don't think slowly and carefully about what is going to happen as a result of what they are doing. They don't take the time to make predictions about what the consequences of their acts will be. As I am sure you can easily guess, people who are impulsive—people who don't think of future consequences—get into a lot of trouble.

Impulsive people often think only about the pleasure of the moment. They only think about how good they feel about what they're doing, and they don't think about the future pains they may suffer because of their impulsivity. They say they'll worry about the future in the future. This is a very bad idea. Such people often end up in a lot of trouble.

SUFFERING PAIN IN THE PRESENT TO AVOID PAINFUL CONSEQUENCES IN THE FUTURE

Often, it's necessary to suffer pain in the present in order to have pleasure in the future. For example, no infant likes to get shots from the doctor. If you were to ask the infant's opinion on the subject it would probably say (if it could) that it doesn't want to get its shots. But these shots are very important because they protect the child from many different kinds of terrible diseases. Even the child's mother feels bad about the

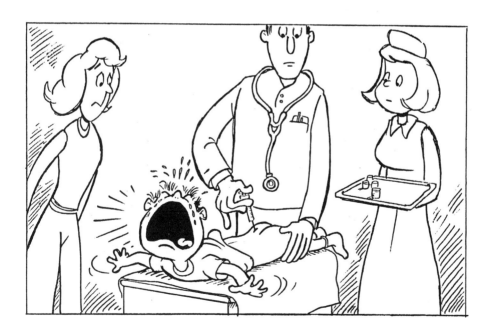

child's receiving shots. But she knows it's important if the child is to be healthy in the future.

Now I will give you another example of how a person may choose to suffer pain in the present in order to enjoy good consequences in the future. A boy would much prefer to watch his favorite television program than to memorize his multiplication tables. However, his teacher has announced a math test for the next day. Even though he has to miss his television program, he decides that it is smarter to study. The next day he gets a very high mark on his test. This boy gave up pleas-

ures in the present in order to enjoy pleasure in the future. He had some pain in the present, the mild pain of studying, in order to enjoy the future pleasure. Most would agree that this boy made a wise decision.

THE FOUR PARTS OF CONCENTRATION

It is important to concentrate in order to prevent impulsivity and bad consequences. Concentration helps a person decide what to do, both in the present and the future. It helps a person make good predictions about future consequences. There are four parts to concentration. I will discuss each one of them separately because they are so important.

Stop!

The first part of concentrating is **stopping**. The person must stop what he or she is doing. No action is taken. There is very little movement of the body.

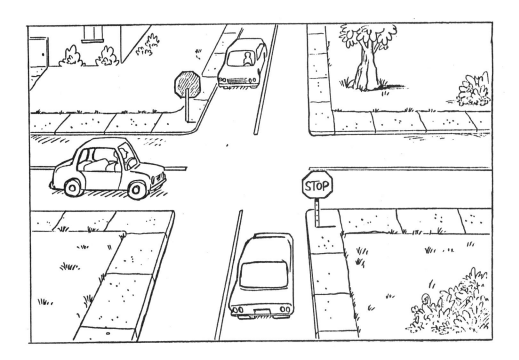

Sometimes people stop and count to 10 before doing something. This is most often very good advice, except in emergencies (like a fire) when counting to 10 might lose important time. This is the reason why we have stop signs on the street. When the cars stop they protect themselves from the consequence of having an accident or hitting a person who is crossing the street.

Look!

The second part of concentration is **looking**. Now the person must use his or her eyes. Here we carefully look to see what is going on all around. Here we get information that **helps** us decide what to **do** (which I will talk about later). The more information we have about a situation, the better we can deal with it. This is why people in cars look all around after they have stopped at a stop sign. After people stop their cars, they look all around to see whether there is any danger.

They look to the left. They look straight ahead. And they look to the right. They also look through the rear-view mirror to see what's going on behind them. And, if they are good drivers, they will also look out through both of the rear-view mirrors on each side of the car.

Listen!

The third part of concentration is **listening**. Now the person must use his or her ears. Here we carefully listen to what is going on. In this way, we get even more information that helps us decide what to do. As I have said before, the more information we have about a situation, the better we can deal with it.

This is what a driver does when stopping in front of railroad tracks. When people stop at railroad signals,

they not only see the red lights flashing, but they also hear the loud bell which warns them that a train is coming. They also listen for the train whistle, which is another warning. People who stop at a railroad crossing, then, stop, look, and listen. The information they get helps them protect themselves from the danger of the train.

Think!

The fourth part of concentration is **thinking**. Here we think about all the information we got from stopping, looking, and listening. This information helps us decide what to do. While thinking, a person is not being impulsive. In a way, concentration is the opposite of impulsivity.

When thinking about what to do, an important thing to think about is future consequences. The person may say to himself or herself: "If I do this, something bad will happen. However, if I don't do that, then the bad thing won't happen." Or the person might say: "If I do this, a good thing will happen. If I don't do this, then the good thing won't happen." The more we concentrate—the longer we stop, look, listen, and think—the more information we get and the better will be our prediction about future consequences. And this is what happens when a person stops a car at a railroad crossing. While the car is just sitting there, the person sees the flashing red stop lights, hears the clanging bells, and hears the oncoming train. This is all important information for a person to have in order to make a smart decision. The person then thinks: "I'd better not drive my car yet. If I do, I might get hit by the train." The person here is thinking of future consequences.

DOING OR NOT DOING

The purpose of the four parts of concentration is to help the person decide what to do, that is, what action if any to take. Sometimes the person will decide that it is best to **do something**, and sometimes the person will decide that it is best to **do nothing**. It depends upon the situation. But before people can make smart decisions, they must remember to stop, look, listen, and think!

It may seem to you that the four parts of concentration will take a long time. This is not necessarily so. The more you do it, the more you practice, the more quickly you can do the four parts. People who skip the four parts of concentration—who do not stop, look, listen, and think—are impulsive and they get into a lot of trouble. People who do stop, look, listen, and think do not get into as much trouble and have much better lives.

Doing or Taking Action

As I have said, after thinking about all the information, the person can decide one of two things: to do something or not to do something. Here, I will talk about situations in which the person decides to do something. That is also called taking action. Later, I will talk about situations in which the person decides not to do something. Both are important. It is also important for a person to decide in advance which he or she will do, something or nothing.

When a person decides—after concentrating—to do something, there will usually be two or more choices. There are many possible things to do and the person has to decide which one to do. What the person does is called a **plan of action**. One way of deciding which plan of action to choose is to think about the consequences of each plan. That is probably the best way to decide which plan of action to take. Remember again that one good choice may be to do nothing. Many people who get into trouble don't think about that choice seriously. It is the choice that says, "Stay away from trouble." Later I will talk about the choice of doing nothing. Here I will be talking about the choice of doing something.

Before giving you some examples of taking action, I want to say a few things about the word **reputation**. The word reputation is an important one. It means what people usually think of you. For example, a boy may study very hard and most often get high grades. He will get the reputation of being a good student. Another boy may get the reputation of being good at sports. But another may have the reputation of being a liar, cheat, or thief. I hope you don't have any of these bad reputations.

Once a person has a bad reputation, it may be very hard to change it to a good reputation. Usually, a person can't change a bad reputation by doing one good thing. Usually, the person must do many good things—over a long time—before the reputation will change. Also, people with bad reputations sometimes get blamed for doing bad things, even when they are innocent. If they are nearby when the trouble happened, everybody thinks they were involved—even if they weren't. This is one of the extra problems that people with bad reputations have. Now that you understand what the word reputation means you will be able to understand better the examples I give here about doing and taking action.

David often got into trouble in school. However, he always had an excuse to try to convince people that he was innocent. He was always saying that the other person started the trouble. His parents and teachers were always telling him to "stay away from trouble," but he always seemed to be involved when there was trouble.

David had a reputation for being a troublemaker. One day, while in the schoolyard, he saw Tom grab Robert's book and then run away with it. Robert was as big as Tom, could run as fast as Tom, and was able to take care of himself and fight his own battles. As David watched Robert running after Tom, he decided that Robert needed his help. Without concentrating, without thinking about future consequences, he impulsively ran after Tom, jumped on him, and dragged him to the ground. The teacher saw what David had done and sent him immediately to the principal.

Later, when David explained that he was only trying to help Robert, both the teacher and principal

did not accept his excuse. They tried to tell him that he should have "minded his own business." His mother was asked to come to school in order to bring him home. His mother and father then punished him by making him spend the rest of the day and evening alone in his room.

You may be wondering what happened to Tom, the boy who took Robert's book. Well, Tom did not have the reputation of being a troublemaker. Most often he was good. However, he was certainly being bad when he grabbed Robert's book. Therefore, the principal warned him to be very careful and not to get into any more trouble. He told him that if he did, then his parents would have to come to school to take him home and they would probably punish him also.

It was sad for David that he didn't stop, look, listen, and think. If he had, he could have thought of the choice of doing nothing. And he could have predicted that if he jumped on Tom, he would get into trouble. He might also have thought about his bad reputation, and about how people with the reputation of being trouble-makers are more likely to be punished than those, like Tom, who are good most of the time.

Jane's teacher told the class that there was going to be a very important test the next day. The test was going to cover all the work of the month before. She told everybody that it was going to be a very hard test and that it was important to spend a lot of time studying. Jane was very upset because she had planned to watch her favorite television program that evening.

After supper she began to think hard about what to do. First, she thought about what might happen if she watched the program. She would enjoy it, but she might get a low grade on her test. Then she thought about studying and getting a high grade.

Then she thought about a third possibility, namely, that she would enjoy the program and have a lot of fun watching it. Then, by **good luck**, the test would be very easy and she would get a very high grade. But then she remembered what the teacher had said about the test being very hard. So she quickly decided that that wasn't going to happen.

Then she thought about how the pleasure of a high grade would be greater than the pleasure of the TV program. She realized also that the pain associated with her not watching her TV program would be less than the pain of getting a low grade on the test.

Now Jane was concentrating. She stopped before doing anything, and she thought slowly and carefully. She thought about all the choices, all the plans of action. And, most important, she thought about the future consequences of each plan of action. She finally decided **not** to watch her favorite TV program and study for the test. She was very glad for her decision because she got a very high grade, one of the highest in the class.

Doing Nothing

There are times when the best thing to do is absolutely nothing. One way I give this advice is to say: "Don't do something, just stand there." Many people find this very hard advice to take. They believe that it's very important always to **do** something. People who believe this often get into a lot of trouble. There are times when it's best to do something, and there are also times when it's best to do nothing. Everybody has a choice and there is no good reason why people should limit themselves to one choice when they have two. There are also some people who most often do nothing, who never, or hardly ever **do something**. These people also will have troubles because doing something would have been the best choice. Here I will give some examples of how doing nothing was the best choice.

As you probably remember, the word **reputation** means what most people think about you. You can have a good reputation or a bad reputation. George had a very bad reputation. His was the reputation of the troublemaker. Whenever there was trouble you could be sure that George was involved. And even when he actually wasn't involved, people suspected that he was. And that's what happens to people who have bad reputations. Even when they're innocent they are often considered to be guilty. George had gotten into a lot of trouble because he was impulsive and he had trouble stopping himself from getting involved in problems that were none of his business. His parents and his teachers had told him many times such things as, "Just walk away when you see trouble," "It was none of your business," and "Why don't you just walk away from trouble instead of walking toward it?"

Even though he was punished many times for not taking this advice, George continued to get into trouble. He often had to stay after school because of his troublemaking. Frequently, he was sent to the principal's office. At home, as well, his parents would punish him for his bad behavior in school. Fortunately for George, he gradually came to realize that his parents and teachers were right and that he would be much better off staying away when there was trouble. It wasn't easy for George to do this; in fact it was very hard.

One day, while George was playing in the schoolyard, two younger boys were fighting with an older boy. Before he changed his ways, this was just the kind

of situation in which George would always become involved. He realized, however, that the teacher would see the four boys fighting and that he would once again get punished. Accordingly, although it was very difficult for him to do, George stood there and did nothing. He just watched. While watching, there were times that he wanted very much to join in, but he stopped himself. He controlled his impulsivity, and after a while, just walked away. As you might suspect a teacher came over and sent all three boys to the principal's office. George was then glad that he hadn't gotten involved.

Frank's teacher told the class on Friday that there would be a big test on Monday. Unfortunately for him, Frank spent the whole weekend having fun. He only thought about the fun he was having at that moment and did not think about future consequences. Also, Frank purposely did not tell his parents about the test, and so they didn't even remind him to study.

When the teacher gave out the test on Monday morning, Frank saw that it was very hard. Sitting next to him was Eric, a very good student. Frank thought about whether or not he should copy from Eric's paper. First, he thought it would be a good idea because he might then get a high grade. Then he thought about the teacher's catching him, and giving him a failing grade. He also thought about the other kids' seeing him cheating and calling him a "cheater." He also thought about the fact that if he did then get a high grade, he still wouldn't feel very good about himself, because he didn't deserve the high grade. In his heart he would know that he had cheated.

Here, Frank was concentrating. He stopped, looked around, and then thought about the different choices and the future consequences of each. He was certainly not being impulsive. Had he been impulsive he proba-

bly would have copied from Eric. He was really concentrating, although all these different thoughts ran quickly through his head. He finally decided that he wouldn't cheat and that the painful consequences of being caught cheating were greater than the painful consequences of a low grade.

He took the test and got a low grade. But this disappointment helped him remember to study hard the next time. And this is exactly what happened. The next time the teacher announced a test, Frank realized that it was important to give up **some** of his fun in order to study. He realized, also, that he didn't have to give up all of his fun, because you don't have to study all the time. There is still time for play.

Gail was always trying to act like a big shot. She was always trying to act older than she really was. Although she was still in grade school, she thought it was "cool" to act like the older children in junior, and even senior high school. One day, Gail came to school with a package of cigarettes. The cigarettes were hidden in her book bag. She asked some of her friends to join her after school and smoke them behind the school building. Lots of her friends thought that would be very exciting and told her that they would be there.

Doris was one of Gail's friends. She had mixed feelings about smoking cigarettes. One part of her wanted to go along with the crowd and keep up with what the others were doing. She didn't want to be singled out or looked at as different from the others. However, she also knew that cigarettes were very unhealthy and that you could get cancer and other diseases if you smoked a lot of them. She heard about people getting "hooked" on cigarettes so that once they started they could not stop. However, because she didn't want to look different from the others she told Gail that she would be there.

Throughout the rest of the school day Doris thought a lot about the cigarette smoking. She thought about the reasons for joining her friends and the reasons for not joining them. She realized that if she joined them she would be one of the crowd and would not have to feel bad about being different from the others. However, she was also frightened that she would get caught and be punished. She thought about the various sicknesses that you can get and how terrible her parents and teachers would feel if they learned what she had done. Finally, although it was very difficult for her to do, she told Gail that she had changed her mind and that she wouldn't be joining them. Gail and her friends tried to get her to go and said that she was "a baby" and a "scaredy cat" because she didn't want to smoke cigarettes. But Doris did not get weaker. She said to her friends: "Cigarette

smoking is bad. You can get many diseases from it. If you get caught you're going to get into a lot of trouble. I'm going home." This was very hard for Doris to do, but she knew it was right. Doris had stopped and thought. She wasn't impulsive. She thought of future consequences. And she felt much better about herself after she left, even though she knew that some of the girls might be angry at her.

IMPORTANT THINGS TO REMEMBER

1. The best way to deal with a problem is to concentrate on it: to stop, look, listen, and think.
2. Don't be impulsive. Think of future consequences before you act.

3. Think of all your choices and then think about the actions you can take that will give you the greatest pleasure, or the least trouble, in the future.

4. Think about the possibility of doing nothing at all. Sometimes that is better than doing something.

CHAPTER 7

Fight and Flight, Anger and Fear

WHAT ARE FIGHT AND FLIGHT?

I am sure that most of you know what **fighting** is. When people fight they may yell and scream and even hit each other. The opposite of the word **fight** is **flight**. A person who runs away from a fight is said to be in **flight**. We also say that that person is **fleeing**. We can learn a lot about fight and flight by studying the behavior of animals. In fact what we learn from animals about fight and flight can be useful for children and adults.

WHAT IS SURVIVAL?

The word **survival** has to do with staying alive. To survive is the opposite of to die. A person whose life is in danger may get out of the trouble and then stay alive. We say that that person has survived. If, however, the person is killed, we say that the person died, or in other words, that the person did not survive.

USING FIGHT OR FLIGHT TO SURVIVE

Fight and flight are necessary for survival. Without them animals, including people, would be less likely to survive. Sometimes, fighting is the best way to survive; sometimes fleeing is the best way to survive. I will now give you some examples of how animals use either fight or flight to survive.

The Wolf and the Rabbit

In the forest a wolf runs after a rabbit. Because the wolf is so much bigger and stronger than the rabbit, the

rabbit runs away as fast as it can. Everyone would agree that it would be a very stupid thing for the rabbit to try to fight the wolf. If it did, it would be eaten up very quickly. Also, the animals who are watching this do not laugh at the rabbit for running away. They do not call the rabbit "chicken" or "scaredy cat." In fact, they think that the rabbit is doing a very smart thing by running away. And, if the rabbit were to try to fight the wolf, they would probably think it was crazy.

There are people, however, who think that running away is always a bad thing. They think that only cowards run away. I do not agree with such people. I think that running away can, at times, be a very smart thing. In such situations to do the opposite, to fight, is a very stupid thing.

The Wise-Guy and the Twins

Victor was the class wise-guy. He was a big shot and a show-off. One day he came to school with a Boy Scout knife and started acting tough with it. In the schoolyard he met Adam and Bernie, who were twin brothers. He pointed the knife at the two boys and told them that if they didn't give him money he would stab them. Adam immediately ran away to tell the teacher. As he started to run Victor called him a scaredy cat. Bernie, however, didn't want to be called a scaredy cat. He thought that everybody would laugh at him for running away. So he tried to fight with Victor and grabbed the knife. Unfortunately, Victor was stronger than Bernie and, while fighting, Bernie got cut. By that time the teacher came. First, she took Bernie to the nurse's office. The nurse took him to a nearby hospital, where he had to have seven stitches. Then the teacher

took Victor to the principal's office. The principal called in Victor's parents and told them that he could not come back to school for two weeks and he suggested that they bring Victor to a therapist.

After that, nobody laughed at Adam for running away. When they saw what happened to Bernie, they knew that Adam had done the smart thing. Everybody thought that Victor had a "screw loose in his head" and that he had done a terrible thing. The important point here is that most people thought that Adam did a smart thing by running away. In certain situations running away is the smart thing and fighting is the stupid thing.

The Ostrich and the Lion

The ostrich is the biggest bird in the whole world. He is even bigger than most grown-ups. Ostriches often live in places where there are lions. The places where ostriches and lions live often have grass, sand, and low bushes—but not too many trees. Therefore, the ostrich can be seen from far away. By lying on its belly, behind the bushes and grass, the ostrich can hide from dangerous animals—animals such as lions. The ostrich also has very good eyesight.

Therefore, when an ostrich sees a lion in the distance it will get down on its belly and hide behind the bushes. The ostrich hopes that it was not seen by the lion. Because it has very good eyesight it can watch the lion very carefully. While the ostrich is lying there it

thinks about whether it should fight or flee. I do not believe that the ostrich would be ashamed of itself if it decided to run away. It is not like many people who believe there is something to be ashamed of if they have to flee.

Sometimes, the lion will run toward the ostrich in order to eat it. Although the ostrich is a very large bird, its wings are not too big, and so it cannot fly high in the air. Therefore, unlike other birds, it could not fly so high that it would be out of the lion's reach. It could not fly up to the top of a high tree and escape. However, the ostrich is one of the fastest runners of all the animals. Therefore, if given enough time, it can often escape from the lion.

If, however, the ostrich doesn't get away in time it will fight the lion in order to survive. Fortunately, the ostrich is a very good fighter. It has very strong legs with two very large toes on each foot. These toes are like claws. In a fight the ostrich's toenails can rip open a lion's skin. The ostrich has very strong legs and its kicks can be very painful to the lion. Also, it can make very loud frightening noises when it fights and this can scare the lion as well.

Some people think that ostriches hide their heads in the sand when there is danger. This is not true. An

ostrich would never do such a stupid thing. Either it runs away in order to save its life and therefore survive, or it fights in order to save its life and therefore survive.

People can also stop and think about whether they want to fight or flee. People should give themselves the choice.

The Firesetter in the School Bathroom

Max thought it was great fun to light fires. One day he went into the school bathroom and began setting fire to rolls of toilet paper. Obviously, Max was a boy with terrible problems. As he was doing this Dan and

151

José came into the bathroom. Dan immediately jumped on Max in order to get the matches away from him and to stop him from lighting more fires. José was quite scared and decided to run to the principal's office immediately. The principal got a couple of teachers and they managed to put out the fires before they spread. Then, the principal called Max's parents to school and told them that he could not return to school and he would have to go to a special hospital where they treated disturbed children who were dangerous. In this situation **both** things were the right things to do. Dan did the right thing by fighting with Max in order to stop him from lighting more fires. And José did the right thing by running to the principal's office for help. This is a good example of how either fight or flight can be the right thing to do.

The Fox and the Chicken

Farmers usually worry about foxes getting into their chicken coops. Foxes like to eat chickens and it is very hard for a chicken to defend itself against a fox. Therefore, farmers try to build very good fences around the places where their chickens are. Also, they try to make sure that the chicken coops, the houses where the chickens live, also have very good walls so that foxes and other animals cannot get inside and eat the chickens. In spite of all these attempts to protect the chickens, foxes and other animals sometimes do succeed in getting into chicken coops and eating the chickens.

This is what happened one day at Farmer Gordon's farm. A fox got into the chicken coop and began

chasing the chickens. All the chickens tried to flee because they knew that it would be very hard to fight and beat a fox. One chicken ran to the corner of the coop and the fox thought that would be a good chicken to catch because it was trapped in the corner. The chicken could not run away because it was trapped. Because this chicken in the corner could no longer flee, it had no choice but to fight. Accordingly, it tried to peck and scratch the fox. The chicken hoped that it

might scratch out the fox's eyes or wound it with its claws. The chicken jumped up and down and thrashed its claws around wildly. Fortunately for the chicken it was able to scratch one of the foxes eyes. The fox then ran away because it knew that if it stayed its other eye might get scratched also.

154

This is a good example of how running away is the best thing to do at first. However, when you can't run away and you are trapped, fighting may be the only thing to do. Fighting the fox helped the chicken survive. The chicken would have run away if it could. However, it was trapped in the coop and couldn't. So, it did the only thing left, it fought. And it fought very hard. And in this case the fighting worked. The chicken saved its life and the fox ran away.

The Mean Old Lady and the German Shepherd

Mrs. Simpson was a mean old lady. She lived alone near a school. She owned a big German shepherd, which was a very angry dog. She seemed to enjoy getting the dog to scare children. And the dog seemed to enjoy snarling and barking at children. All of the children were frightened of Mrs. Simpson and her dog. They complained to their parents, teachers, and the principal—but nothing could be done about it. The law was on her side. She was entitled to have her dog and, as long as the dog didn't bite anybody, she was allowed to keep it. When the principal sent her a letter asking her to please stop scaring the children with her dog she wrote him back a letter in which she said, "It's a free country and mind your own business."

Therefore, the children stayed away from her house and would walk on the other side of the street. Sometimes, when a new child came to the school, and didn't know about Mrs. Simpson and her dog, he or she would walk on her side of the street. However, as soon as the dog barked the child would run away. This is a good example of a situation in which the smartest thing to do is to avoid trouble and to run away when you are close to it. Mrs. Simpson was mean and she had a mean dog. It would be foolish of a child to try to fight the dog. Therefore, the best thing to do is to stay away from the dog and avoid trouble.

As you can see, people, like animals, have a choice of whether they should fight or flee. Sometimes it's better to fight and sometimes it's better to flee. There's nothing to be ashamed of if you have to fight, if you're forced into fighting. But you shouldn't be the one to start fights. Also, there is nothing to be ashamed of if you have to flee. However, you shouldn't be the one to start doing things to others that would make them flee.

WHAT ARE ANGER AND FEAR?

Anger and **fear** are feelings. Another word for **feelings** is **emotions**. Just as fight and flight are useful for survival, so are anger and fear. Anger is a feeling that helps you fight better. Fear is a feeling that helps you flee faster. We fight harder and better when we are angry and we run faster when we are frightened. Therefore, they both help survival. First I will talk about anger and then I will talk about fear.

ANGER

Anger is the feeling we get when we want something that we cannot have, or that we think we cannot have. Anger has a use. It helps you try to get what you want, or think you want. Sometimes it works and you get what you want. Sometimes it doesn't work and you don't get what you want. If anger is successful and you get the thing you want, then you are no longer angry. If you don't get the thing you want, then you may still be angry. And anger that stays inside you, that keeps rumbling within you, makes you feel bad about yourself. It lowers self-esteem and can cause other troubles. Therefore, it's best to let your anger out and use it in the best possible way. Now I will talk about the different ways of letting out anger.

Using Your Anger to
Get the Thing You Want

The best way to use anger is to let it out when you first realize that you are angry. At that time, there is usually only a small amount of anger to let out. If you don't let it out then it may build up into bigger amounts of anger. Then, when large amounts of anger are let out, it may cause you a lot of trouble. Also, it is important to use it in the right way, not in a way that is going to get everyone around you very upset.

157

The way David and Ben handled the situation with their babysitter, Flora, is a good example of the right way to use anger. Soon after the boys' parents would leave, Flora would get on the phone and talk to her teenage friends. When the boys would ask her to play with them, she would say, "I'm busy. I'll be with you later." This made the boys very angry because they

wanted Flora to play with them. They waited awhile and hoped that Flora would get off the phone soon. But she still stayed on the phone.

Then David went over to her and said, "I'm going to tell my mommy on you. You're supposed to watch us. You're supposed to play with us."

But Flora still didn't get off the phone. Instead, she said, "I'm talking with my boyfriend. He's more important than you. If you don't stop bothering me I'm going

158

to tell your mother that you've both been bad and then she'll punish you."

This got the boys even angrier. But they knew that Flora was just not going to play with them because she was more interested in talking with her boyfriend. They decided that they would tell their parents as soon as they could. Just thinking about telling their parents made them less angry.

Later on, after Flora finally got off the phone, the telephone rang. It was the boys' mother. It was David who picked up the phone and his mother said to him, "What's been going on there? I've been trying to get through for two hours. Who's been on the phone?"

David answered: "Mommy, it was Flora. She was talking with her boyfriend and she just wouldn't get off the phone. We begged her to play with us and she wouldn't. She said that her boyfriend was more important than us." The mother said, "Let me speak with Flora."

David put Flora on the phone. First she tried to deny that she was on the phone. She tried to make up some story about the phone being broken. The mother then told Flora that both parents were coming home immediately. And, when they came home, they discussed this further with Flora and she finally admitted that she had been on the phone all that time. The boys' father took Flora home and they never used her as a babysitter again. They then got a new babysitter who spent a lot of time playing with the boys and they had a lot of fun together. The boys were happy that they

had told everyone how angry they were. By telling their parents what was bothering them they changed the thing that was getting them angry. Then the problem was solved and they were no longer angry.

The Substitute

One way of getting rid of anger is to get a **substitute**. A substitute is getting something instead of the thing you want. For example, when your teacher is absent another teacher comes in to teach the class. The new teacher is called a substitute. You may not like the second teacher as much as your own, but that teacher is still better than no teacher at all.

This is how a substitute works to lessen anger. Kate wanted a puppy very much. Many of her friends had pets and she wanted one also. But, when she asked her parents to buy her one, they refused. They said that pets are a lot of trouble and that they couldn't trust Kate to take care of a dog. Kate kept asking them, and they kept saying no. This made her very angry. Each

time they said no she got even angrier. One day, when Kate was particularly upset about not getting a pet, her parents asked her how she would feel about getting a hamster. They said that the hamster would be a substitute for a dog. They told her that they wouldn't mind a hamster, because a hamster doesn't have to be walked at night and is much less trouble to take care of. Kate said that she thought a dog would be much more fun, but, if she couldn't have a dog, she would certainly like to have a hamster.

So they bought a hamster and Kate found that it was a lot of fun. After a few days she loved the hamster very much and spent a lot of time with it. We see here how getting something else, a substitute, can help anger go away. We see here also how Kate's anger helped her get something.

Changing Your Mind
About the Thing You Want

Another way of getting rid of anger is to change your mind about the thing you want. If you stop wanting the thing, you'll no longer be angry. Often, talking to other people about the thing you want may help you change your mind about it. However, if you don't say anything, you might not change your mind and then you'll still be angry.

Harriet and Isabelle were stepsisters. Their parents had divorced and then Harriet's mother married Isabelle's father. During the week Harriet lived with her mother, but she visited with her father every other weekend. Also, during the week Isabelle lived with her father, but she visited with her mother every other weekend. Therefore, during the week the two girls lived together. They also lived together on those weekends when both were not visiting the other parents. Before the divorces they had been only children. Now, they were sisters. Both were very happy about this, because before the new marriage each was very lonely.

However, there was a problem. They shared the same bedroom. In the first marriages, each had her own room. Although each was happy to have a sister, each was unhappy about sharing the room. At times they would get very angry with one another. They felt cramped in this room. They didn't like sharing the space. Sometimes they even felt as if they were in the same jail cell.

Both of them complained to their parents about how angry they were living in that one room together. However, their parents told them that there was nothing they could do about it. They did not have enough money to buy a bigger house where there would be a room for each child. After a while, they realized that their parents were right and that there was nothing they could do about the situation. When they stopped wishing for separate rooms—something they couldn't have—they then became less angry. Finally, they were not angry at all. In fact, sometimes it was even nice living in the same room, especially at night, when they would cuddle together in bed.

Accepting the Fact That You Can't Have the Thing You Want

Another way of getting rid of anger is to accept the fact that you can't have what you want. This is also called **resignation**. When you **resign** yourself to the fact that you can't have the thing you want, you will be less angry about it. When you stop thinking about the thing, you will no longer be angry. Another way of saying this is, "Forget about it! You can't have it! So there's nothing to be gained by eating your heart out over the fact that you can't have it." The more you think about the thing you can't have, the more you'll be miserable. If you accept the fact that you can't have it you'll no longer be miserable.

Eve's parents used to fight a lot. As time passed, they fought more and more. Finally, they told her that they were going to get a divorce. This made Eve very angry. She begged them to change their minds, but they refused. They told her that they had tried very hard to solve their problems, but they couldn't. They too were very sad about the divorce. Even though Eve begged them very hard to change their minds, they refused.

After that, Eve's father left the house, and Eve remained living in the house with her mother. She spoke to her father practically every day and visited with him once and sometimes twice a week. During all this time she kept hoping that they would get married again. But they didn't. When she would ask her father if he would ever marry her mother again he answered, "Eve, I've told you many times that it just won't happen. The more you keep wishing for your mother and me to marry again, the more miserable and angry you're going to be."

When she asked her mother if she would marry her father again, her mother answered: "Eve, I wish you'd just forget about it. I'm **never** going to marry your father again. We just can't live together. He's a good man, and I'm a good woman, but we're no good together. Why don't you just accept the fact that it's never going to happen?'' Sometimes, after her parents would speak this way, Eve would cry. At other times, she would have angry temper tantrums. But this didn't work either. It took a long time, but she finally accepted the fact that they were **never** going to marry again. And when this finally happened, she was less sad and less angry. She stopped begging them to marry again, she stopped having crying spells, and she stopped having temper tantrums. Her anger went away when she resigned herself to the fact that her parents would never marry again.

Hitting Things Is Not a Good Way to Get Rid of Anger

There are some people who believe that if you are angry about something the best way to get rid of the anger is to hit something, and even scream and shout while you are doing that. This is a very silly idea. It just doesn't work. Hitting something doesn't change the trouble that caused the anger in the first place.

What happened with Amy and her kite one day is a good example of this. Her parents had bought her a new kite and she was quite excited. It was a very windy day, a perfect day for flying kites. Amy ran with her kite, and up, up, up it went—high in the sky. Amy was very excited. But then, as she was running with the kite, it suddenly got caught in the top of a high tree. Instead of gently pulling the string, she pulled it very hard. The string then broke and soon afterwards the kite was blown away from the top of the tree. It kept going far, far away. Amy stood there and watched the kite until it looked so small that she could no longer see

166

it. Amy began to cry. She was sad and angry at the same time. Then she started to jump up and down and

scream. Amy's teenage brother heard her crying and screaming. After Amy told him what had happened her brother said, "Why don't you just throw rocks at that tree? That will make you feel better." So Amy got some rocks and started throwing them at the tree. She also called the tree bad names. And her brother also picked up some rocks and started throwing them at the tree. And he too started calling the tree bad names. Although this made Amy feel a little better, she was still very sad and angry. She still could not stop thinking about her kite. Then, as they were still throwing rocks

at the tree, their father came home and asked the children what they were doing. They explained to him that Amy's kite blew away, that she was very angry about it, and that throwing rocks was going to help Amy feel less angry.

Their father then said: "I don't think that's going to work very well. Although you may feel a little less sad and angry, you still don't have your kite. No matter how many rocks you throw at that tree, you are still not going to have a kite. The best way to feel less angry about your lost kite is to get another kite." He then asked Amy if she had enough money to buy a kite. She went to her piggy bank and saw that she only had half the amount of money she needed to buy a kite. Her father then added the amount that she needed, and she bought a new kite. Then, she was no longer angry.

WHAT IS THE RIGHT AMOUNT
OF ANGER TO LET OUT?

Some people hold in their anger and do not let out any at all, or almost none at all. This is not a good thing to do. There are others who let out too much. This is not a good thing either. The best thing to do is to let out just the right amount, not too little and not too much. Here I will talk about these three kinds of people.

People Who Don't
Let Out Enough Anger

There are some people who are very afraid to say that they are angry. They keep all their anger bottled up inside. No matter how many things there are that

169

get them angry, no matter how many things they want that they can't have, they say nothing about it. This is a very bad idea. People who do this do not get the things they want. They just build up anger inside themselves and feel miserable. They may have a very strange idea. They may believe that people who are angry are bad and even sinful. They may even have been taught such a thing by their parents or other adults.

Carl's parents were divorced. He was an only child. He lived with his mother, and his father would visit some of the weekends. I say **some** because he was supposed to come one day of every weekend, but he didn't. Sometimes his father would be late, and sometimes his father would not even show up at all. His father was very inconsiderate. That means that he wouldn't even call in

advance to tell Carl and his mother that he was going to be late, or that he wasn't going to show up at all. But Carl was afraid to say anything to his father. He was scared that if he told his father how angry he was about his being late that he might see even less of his father. And so he said nothing. And his father kept missing visits and being late.

If Carl had spoken up and told his father how angry he was, one of two things might have happened. Perhaps his father would have realized how inconsiderate he was. He might then try to be on time and not miss visits. Then, Carl would have used his anger to change something that was bothering him. He would then be happy that he had let it out, told his father how he felt, and changed the thing that was bothering him. If he had done this he would have also raised his self-esteem. Holding in anger lowers self-worth. Letting out the right amount—in a way that changes things that bother you—raises self-worth.

The other thing that might have happened is that his father would still continue to be late and miss visits. Even though he had told his father, even though he had let out his angry feelings, this still hadn't worked to change the thing that was bothering him. However, even if the second thing happened, Carl could at least say to himself that he had tried. And then, he might even be a little less angry because he had at least tried to do something about it. He might then give up trying, resign himself to the fact his father might not come, and do other things—substitute things that would make him happy. Then he would probably be even less angry.

There is an old saying: **Nothing ventured, nothing gained**. I believe that this is one of the wisest of all the old proverbs. This old saying means that if you don't try you won't accomplish anything. If you do try, you may get something. If you don't try, you're just where you were before, often nowhere. If you do try, you may get what you want and then you'll feel better. If you don't try you just remain miserable. I hope you will always remember this wise saying.

People Who Let Out Too Much Anger

There are some people who are just the opposite. When they get angry they scream, shout, and have temper tantrums. They may throw things and break things. They may have fits. They may rave and rant. Although such people are letting everybody know how angry they are, they generally make things much worse for themselves, not better. Although they are letting out their anger, they are causing new troubles that they didn't have before. People who act this way get everybody around them angry and then they get new problems in addition to those that may have originally gotten them angry. People who have this problem often don't realize that they are making things much worse for themselves, rather than better.

This was one of Wendy's problems. When she was younger, whenever she wanted something, she would rant and rave until her parents finally gave in and gave her what she wanted. This was not a very smart thing for her parents to do. They should have told her that such fits just won't work and they weren't going to give her everything she wanted. Wendy knew that if she screamed long enough and hard enough her parents would finally give her whatever she wanted. As a result she became a spoiled brat.

When Wendy would visit her friend's house, she would also have temper tantrums when she didn't get what she wanted. Her friend's parents, however, would not give in to Wendy when she would have these tantrums. Rather, they would tell her that she had to go home. Not only did friends stop inviting her over, but

she had trouble in school because of her outbursts. The teacher gave her bad reports in classroom behavior and her parents often had to come to school. Therefore, if you are angry about something tell the people at whom you are angry in a nice, polite way. If you don't, and have tantrums instead, you will just make things worse, and you won't get what you want.

People Who Let Out Just the Right Amount of Anger

The best way to deal with anger is to speak about it when you first start to be angry. The best way is to talk about it—using polite words—with the people with whom you are angry. It is best to do this very early, before it builds up. If it builds up inside you, and you don't let it out, you will feel bad about yourself. It will rumble and grumble inside you for a long time, and this will lower your self-esteem. Also, you won't do anything to change what's causing you to be angry in the first place. If it builds too much you may then explode and have the kinds of tantrums that got Wendy into so much trouble. You will then be like a volcano that explodes after the lava, rocks, mud, and other stuff have been kept inside for a long time. Then it all comes out at once. The best thing is to let the anger out early, when there is only a small amount to let out. When you use polite words you can even have some angry feelings with them, but not big angry feelings or tantrums. When you show a little angry feeling, people get the idea that what they are doing has bothered you. And this is a good thing to do.

Ed joined Little League. He was very excited. He loved to play baseball and he was glad to be old enough to join. Many of his friends were on the team, including George. George was the son of the coach, Mr. Johnson. Ed knew that he could not play in every inning and that everybody had to have a chance to play. However, he and some of the other boys began to notice that the coach was letting his son, George, play much more than the others. The boys talked about it, but were afraid to say anything because they thought the coach might get angry at them.

But Ed was angry and so he told the coach what was bothering him. Although he was angry, he did not have a temper tantrum. He used polite words and did not use any dirty words. Mr. Johnson listened carefully to what Ed was saying and then said to him: "Ed,

you're right. I didn't realize that I was giving George more time. I guess I was doing that because he's my son. But what I did wasn't right, and I'm going to stop doing that right now. From now on everybody gets an equal chance. Thanks for telling me about this."

Ed was very happy that he had spoken up. The other boys thanked him also. And even George wasn't angry, because he knew that what his father was doing wasn't right. Also, the boys had become angry at George and that didn't make him feel good either. After that, everybody's self-esteem got higher—Ed's, George's, and even Mr. Johnson's. Ed's self-esteem got higher because he had spoken up and used his anger to solve a problem. He then felt good about what he had done. George's self-esteem got higher because the other boys on the team were no longer angry at him for playing more than they. And Mr. Johnson's self-esteem got higher because he stopped doing an unfair thing, and because the boys then liked him more. This is a good example of how telling about your anger very early, before it builds up into tantrums, is the best way to use it.

GROWLING AND BARKING

I have spoken already about dirty words. Before speaking more about them I would like to tell you a little bit about growling and barking. As you know, this is what many animals do. I am sure that most of you have seen dogs that growl and bark. Growling is also called snarling. Growling and barking have a purpose. They let another animal know that the snarling animal is angry. They are a warning. They tell the other animal that it will be in trouble if it doesn't go away. Animals often growl before they fight. The growl may scare the other animal away. The snarl and bark, then, serves the purpose of protecting an animal from attack. It is almost as if the growling or barking animal is saying to the other one: "I'm not scared of you. You'd better get out of here. If you don't, you're going to be in big trouble. If you don't stop bothering me I'm going to attack you, bite you, kill you, and even eat you up."

The Jenkins family had a watchdog named Rover. He was a very smart dog, and the family felt very safe when they left him in the house. One night, while the family was away, a thief climbed into a window at the back of the house. He wanted to steal as many things as he could. As you know, dogs not only smell very well, but can also hear very well. As soon as the robber got into the house, he heard Rover snarling and barking. As fast as he could, the thief jumped out the window. The robber leaped out the window and ran as fast as he could. He was very scared. He knew that the dog's

growls meant that if he didn't get away fast he would be attacked and bitten by the dog. He understood well that the snarling and barking of the dog was a warning, and that he would be in a lot of trouble if he didn't run fast.

Now I want to tell you something else about a dog's snarling and barking. There are many dogs that are not particularly dangerous. In fact, most dogs do not bite people and there is nothing to be afraid of when you are near them. Such dogs may like to growl to scare people, but they really wouldn't do them any harm. About such dogs we often say, "Their bark is worse than their bite."

Lester was walking down the street, when suddenly a dog started running toward him. The dog was growling and barking. The dog was very small and there was really nothing to be afraid of. In fact, the barks were so soft and squeaky that it would be more correct to say that the dog was yapping, rather than barking. Although Lester was a little scared, he just stood there. Lester knew that if he ran the dog would

run after him. He knew also that if he just stood there— even though he was a little scared—the dog would not run after him and would just go away. And Lester was right. After standing there awhile, the dog just walked away. When the dog saw that Lester wasn't afraid of him, it did absolutely nothing. What happened to Lester is a good example of the saying that for some dogs "Their bark is worse than their bite." And this is true of some people also. They may make a lot of noise and try to scare you with their words, but nothing happens if you don't get scared of them.

ANGRY WORDS

Angry words let another person know that you are angry; but they do not harm the other person's body. Angry words are warnings to other people that you are bothered by what they are saying or doing. The angry words let other people know that if they don't stop bothering you, they might get into trouble. Angry words are a little like an animal's growling or snarling. Angry words can therefore be useful because they send a message to other people that you're not just going to stand there and do nothing while they bother you.

Good Angry Words and Bad Angry Words

There are two kinds of angry words: good angry words and bad angry words. Good angry words are regular, polite words—which anyone may use—but can be said in an angry way. Bad angry words are *not* regular, polite words. They are just the opposite. They are also called "dirty words" and "gutter language"— because they belong in the street or gutter, like garbage. Although many people use them, they are not the best way to show anger. Dirty words can be used in many ways. Here I will talk about their use for showing anger.

The best way to show anger is to use good angry words, regular words spoken in such a way that other people know you're angry. When you do this, people are likely to listen to you and try to change the things that are bothering you. When you use bad angry words, that is dirty words, people will usually get very upset with you and you're not likely to get what you want. In fact, when you use such words things will usually get worse.

Many people who use dirty words do so because they don't know many other words to use instead, especially polite words. These other words are called *substitute* words. When your teacher is absent, you get a substitute teacher who teaches instead of your regular teacher. The more words you learn, the more regular, polite words you will be able to use as substitutes. You will then be able to avoid the trouble that children get into when they use gutter language.

Higher Animals and Lower Animals

A little while ago I spoke about dogs who bark and snarl. Dogs and most other animals are called "lower animals." We humans are also animals, but we call ourselves "higher animals." We say this because we believe we are smarter than dogs and other animals and can use our brains better than they. Lower animals can't talk like we can. They can make some sounds, but they can't speak thousands of different words. That's one of the reasons why we say we are higher animals and they are lower. When a lower animal, such as a dog, gets very angry it attacks, bites, and may even kill another animal. When we humans get angry, we do *not* have to do any of these terrible things. We can *talk* about our anger—by using good angry words—and try to solve the problem that way. Lower animals can't talk; we can. Our way is better because it causes no harm to the other person's body.

The more dirty words you use to show anger, the more you are acting like a lower animal. The more polite words you use when you are angry, the more you are acting like a higher animal. Dirty words are like the hissing of a snake and the snarling of a dog. When you use them when you are angry, you are acting like

a lower animal. When you use good angry words when you are angry, you are acting like a higher animal. Which do you want to be? A lower animal or a higher animal?

ANGRY THOUGHTS, ANGRY FEELINGS, AND ANGRY ACTS

Anger has three parts: angry thoughts, angry feelings, and angry acts. Let me tell you about each of these three parts of anger. It is very important to know about the differences among them. If you don't, you may cause yourself a lot of trouble.

Angry Thoughts

Angry thoughts are the things you think about when you are angry. They are in your **mind**. For example, Gail didn't study for a big test in school. She got a very low grade. Even though it was her own fault she was angry at her teacher. She had a thought of hitting her teacher over the head with a hammer. Of

course, she wouldn't really do such a thing. But this was the angry thought that came into her mind.

Angry Feelings

Angry feelings usually go along with angry thoughts. The best way to think about the difference between angry thoughts and angry feelings is to imagine that angry thoughts are mostly in the brain, inside the head; but angry feelings may be all over the body. Angry feelings are also in the brain, but they are in other parts of the body as well. Angry feelings make people's faces change so that they look angry. They may make your heart speed up, make you breathe faster, make your muscles tight and cause you to clench your fists. These are the kinds of changes in your body that make you stronger when you fight. Angry feelings help you fight better. When a dog, or cat, or other animal is ready to fight we can see all these changes in its body. But we don't know exactly what angry thoughts, if any, are in its brain. We guess that the thoughts are like those that we humans have, but we can't be sure. As I said, angry thoughts and angry feelings usually go together.

Angry Acts

Angry acts may come right after angry thoughts and feelings. The **acts** are the things a person **does** about angry thoughts and feelings. It is important to remember that we usually have little or no control over the angry thoughts that may pop into our minds. And we have very little control over the angry feelings that may come over our body. However, we **do** have control over angry acts, the things we may or may not do about our anger. Sometimes it is a good thing to perform an angry act, and sometimes it is a bad thing.

Nat was a sore loser. Whenever he would lose a game he would get very angry and have a big fit. Once, after losing a game of Monopoly, he was very angry. Instead of just being a little sad he got up, banged his fist on the table many times, and then picked up the board and threw it at his friend. His friend was very upset, left the house, and told Nat that he didn't want to play with him any more. This is a good example of an angry act that is not necessary. Nat could have controlled it. He didn't have to be impulsive. After his

friend left he felt very bad. He felt lonely and his self-esteem got very low.

Speaking is one kind of act. When you speak you do something with your mouth and your vocal cords, which are inside your throat. The two together help you speak.

Maria was very angry at Ms. Morales, the basketball coach, for not picking her to be on the basketball team. Maria was so angry at Ms. Morales that she wished she would be hit by a car. However, she didn't tell Ms. Morales what she was thinking. She knew that this would just cause her a lot more trouble. She did, however, tell Ms. Morales that she was very upset and asked her why she wasn't picked to be on the team. Ms. Morales said: "Maria, I know that you could be a very good basketball player. However, during practice times you fool around a lot, giggle with the other girls, and don't pay attention when I teach the children how to

play basketball. I'm sure that if you took the game more seriously you would be good enough to be on the team." And this is exactly what happened. Maria became more serious, listened more carefully to what Ms. Morales was saying at the practice sessions, and she later got on the team. This is a good example of how an angry act can be a good thing to do.

ANGER AND GUILT

As you may remember, guilt is the kind of feeling of low self-worth people have when they have thoughts or feelings or do things that they have learned are bad or wrong. Most people do not feel guilty about their angry thoughts and feelings. Most often such guilt is not necessary. We cannot control our angry thoughts and feelings. Thoughts just pop into our minds and feelings just come over our bodies. We often have no control over them, at least when they are just starting. Angry acts, however, are very different. We **do** have control over them. Nat, the boy who threw the Monopoly set at his friend, had control. He did not have to bang his fist on the table. He should have felt guilty about what he had done.

Some children are taught by their parents that angry thoughts and feelings are very bad to have. Just about every child gets angry at parents, at times. Parents make children do things that they don't like to do—things that may be very good for them to do. They make children eat when they may not want to and do their homework when they may not want to. They make them turn off the television set in the middle of a program, and make them go to sleep earlier than they may wish. All these things make children angry. It is

normal to have angry thoughts and feelings when parents make children do these things. However, there are some parents who make children feel very guilty and bad about themselves when they have such normal thoughts and feelings. Such a parent might say, "What a terrible feeling to have about a parent. You shouldn't even **think** such things." A better thing for a parent to say is: "I can understand how angry you are at me for making you turn off the television and insisting you go to sleep. However, you have to get up early tomorrow to go to school. It's normal for you to have such angry and hateful thoughts and feelings toward me. Have them all you want, but you still have to turn off the television and go to bed." If, however, a child uses dirty words toward a parent, that is, acts on the angry thoughts and feelings, a smart parent should say: "You can think any angry thought you want. You can feel any angry feelings you want. However, I will not permit you to talk that way to me."

If, in addition to angry thoughts and feelings, a child acts out on them by having a temper tantrum, a smart parent should say: "You are not responsible for your angry thoughts, so I won't punish you for them. You are not responsible for your angry feelings, so I won't punish you for them either. However, I'm certainly not going to allow you to pound your fist on the table and break things around here."

Therefore, there's most often nothing to feel guilty about for your angry thoughts and angry feelings. Most often they are normal and they are the same kinds of angry thoughts and feelings that come into anyone's head. Sometimes such thoughts and feelings involve horrible things, like a person getting hit by a car, or a person even dying. It is not that the child really wants these terrible things to happen; it is just that this is the

187

way the mind works. This is the way the mind shows anger. It usually shows anger in a worse way than the person really wants. All this is usually normal. It is only when the person is happy about these terrible things happening, or does something to make these terrible things happen, that the person should feel guilty or ashamed.

ANGRY THOUGHTS AND FEELINGS CANNOT HARM ANYONE

When children are very young they often think that a wish can come true. They may think that simply wishing for something can make it happen. However, as they grow older, they learn that this is not so, and that just thinking about something cannot make it happen. They learn that wishes cannot just simply come true by wishing them. But there are some older children who have not learned this. They still believe that just wishing that something will happen can make it happen. Some of these children believe that thinking angry things can make the things actually happen. The thing would have happened anyway. The wish had nothing to do with the thing happening.

Sometimes a child will have an angry thought or wish and the thing will actually happen. This does not mean that the thoughts made the thing happen. The thing would have happened anyway.

Sam and Vincent were brothers. They were both Cub Scouts. Unfortunately, Sam did not take his homework seriously. One weekend there was a big project to do. He had been told about it three weeks earlier and never did anything about it. On that weekend the Cub Scouts were going off on an overnight hike. Sam's mother did not let him go and made him stay home and do his project. Vincent, however, had done all his homework and was allowed to go. Sam was very angry at Vincent. Instead of blaming himself, he just got more and more angry at Vincent and wished that Vincent would fall off a cliff while he was on the hike. Unfortu-

nately, Vincent did have an accident while on the hike. He didn't actually fall off a cliff, but he did fall down a rocky hill and broke his arm. At first, Sam felt very guilty. He thought that his angry thoughts and feelings, and his wishes that Vincent fall off a cliff, made Vincent have the accident. When he thought that, he felt very guilty. However, later, after talking to his parents about it, he realized that his thoughts did not

harm Vincent and that the two things had nothing to do with one another.

It's important to remember, then, that angry thoughts and feelings cannot harm anyone. They are usually normal and they are not like magic. In fact, there is no such thing as magic. I hope that you are old enough to know this.

FEARFUL THOUGHTS, FEARFUL FEELINGS, AND FEARFUL ACTS

As I have said, just as anger goes with fight, fear goes with flight. When we are angry we fight harder and we are stronger. When we are afraid we run faster and are more likely to protect ourselves from danger. Just as

190

anger has three parts—angry thoughts, angry feelings, and angry acts—fear also has three parts: fearful thoughts, fearful feelings, and fearful acts.

Fearful Thoughts and Fearful Feelings

Fearful thoughts are in the mind, that is, in the brain. Fearful feelings are also in the brain, but they are also in the body. Fearful feelings often go along with fearful thoughts. When you have fearful feelings, your heart beats faster and you breathe more rapidly. You may even get goose pimples on your skin and the little hairs on your arms may stand up a little. Your skin may turn white. Because your heart is beating faster and you are breathing faster, you are able to run more quickly. The more frightened you are the faster you may run. Usually, we cannot control the fearful thoughts that may come into our heads and the fearful feelings that come over our bodies.

Sandra, Frank, and their parents decided one day to take a trip to the beach. When they got there they saw a big sign saying that sharks had been seen in the water earlier that day, and so no one was allowed to go swimming. As the family stood there looking at the sign they had fearful thoughts of shark fins in the water. They also had fearful feelings as they thought about being eaten by sharks. Anyone who would say that this family should not have such fearful thoughts and feelings is foolish. Therefore, in order to protect themselves from the danger of the sharks, the family did not go into the water. Instead, they enjoyed themselves by picnicking on the beach and lying in the sun.

Fearful Acts

Fearful acts come after fearful thoughts and feelings. Although we cannot control the fearful thoughts that come into our minds, and we cannot control the frightened feelings that go along with them, we can control fearful acts. We have control over what we do when we are frightened. Sometimes, the smart thing to do is to fight the fear, not give into it, and not run away or avoid the frightening situation. Other times the good and smart thing to do is to run away as fast as you can.

Sally and her parents were taking a car trip across the United States. One day, as they were driving across the Great Plains, in the central part of the United States, Sally's mother suddenly cried out, "Look over there, it's a tornado!" For those of you who don't know what a tornado is, a tornado is a very strong wind that spins around in circles. The whirling circles of wind are smallest closer to the ground and get larger and larger the higher they are. A tornado moves rapidly along the ground, and destroys and even sucks up most of the things in its path. People can easily get killed by a tornado. Air from all around also gets sucked up by the tornado. This causes very strong, dangerous winds for miles around the tornado. Sure enough, way in the

distance, there was a tornado. Everybody got scared immediately. They couldn't tell whether the tornado was coming toward them or not. However, Sally's father turned the car around and drove as fast as he could in the direction that he thought was away from the tornado. Although the tornado was very far away it was very windy where they were. The air around them was being sucked into the tornado causing strong winds for miles around. The car was shaking and it was very hard for the father to drive in a straight line. Everybody was scared that they would get sucked up by the tornado and might even be killed. Everybody had both fearful thoughts and fearful feelings. Sally's fearful feelings were so strong that her body was shaking. Finally, after they had driven about a half-hour,

they saw that the tornado was going in the opposite direction. But they still kept driving away from it as fast as they could. Then, after another hour, they could no longer see the tornado and they started becoming less frightened. Anybody who would say that this family was foolish for being scared would be saying a stupid thing. Fear helped them protect themselves from danger. It helped them think better about what to do and drive faster. Sally and her parents fleeing the tornado—by driving away as fast as they could—is a good example of running away from a danger. If they hadn't done that, they might have been killed.

Now I'm going to give you an example of a situation in which it was a good thing **not** to run away from a danger, but to fight the fear. Bea's class was going to put on a play. The play was to be Cinderella. Bea's teacher asked her if she would like to play the role of Cinderella. Bea didn't know what to do. She was quite frightened about getting up on the stage all alone with all the people watching her. She was scared that she might forget her part and that everybody would laugh at her. These fears made her want to tell her teacher

that she didn't want to be in the play. However, she also had thoughts of how great it would be if she did a good job and everybody applauded—especially her parents and grandparents. Therefore, Bea had mixed feelings about being in the play. She finally decided to say yes to her teacher, but she knew it wouldn't be easy. She knew she would have to swallow the lump in the

throat that she felt as she got on the stage. She knew that she would have to force herself to do the frightening thing. However, her teacher had told her that such fears are normal and the best thing to do is to fight them and not give in to them. And this is exactly what Bea did. After the play, she was quite proud that she hadn't given in to the fears and turned down the part.

This is a good example of how important it is in life to fight fears. Many new things in life are frightening: The first day of a new school year. Joining a new club like Boy Scouts or Girl Scouts. The first day at sleep away camp. And staying overnight at a new friend's house. The best thing to do is to push yourself to do these things and not give in to the fear of avoiding them. People who do give in to these fears live very lonely and unexciting lives.

There are other times, however, when it is smart to give in to and go along with your scary thoughts and feelings. Good examples would be the families I just spoke about who didn't go into the water because of the danger of sharks and the family that fled the tornado. Such flight can sometimes save a person's life. Other examples would be running away from fires, hiding in the basement during hurricanes, and running away from people who carry dangerous weapons, like knives and guns. Most people would agree that it is stupid not to run when these things happen.

THE COWARD AND
THE BRAVE PERSON

Many people think that the coward and the brave person are exactly opposite from one another. If one looks at what they do, it may very well be that they appear to be different. The brave person fights danger, whereas the coward runs from it. However, in one way they are both the same. I am talking about the fact that they both have the same fears. The difference between them is that cowards usually run when they have fears. Brave people often do not give in to their fears and go ahead and fight or do whatever else they have to do. They try to cover up their fears and do what they have to—even though they are afraid.

The boy who stands still while a dog is barking is being brave. He is covering up his fears. Bea who went on the stage to play Cinderella—even though she was frightened—was being brave. Children who run away from every little frightening thing are acting like cowards. The child who is always too scared to act in a school play is going to miss out on a lot of fun. That child is not going to enjoy the good feelings and high self-esteem that people get when they are standing on a stage and everybody in the audience is clapping. The boy who always runs away from barking dogs is also acting like a coward. I would not call a person a coward who runs away once in a while. I would only call a person a coward who runs away most of the time. People who are brave, who do not give in to their fears, feel good about themselves and are likely to have self-esteem. People who always give in to their fears, and run away most of the time, feel cowardly about themselves and have low self-esteem.

So it's all up to you. You yourself can decide what you do about your fears. You yourself can decide whether you are going to be brave or cowardly. I hope most of you who read this will decide to be brave. Those who do decide to be brave will lead much happier lives and will have many more experiences. Those who are cowardly often are very lonely and do very few things in life.

**IMPORTANT THINGS
TO REMEMBER**

1. Fight and flight are both necessary to protect us from danger.

2. Anger is the feeling that we have when we fight. Anger helps us fight harder and therefore protects us better from danger.

3. Fear is the feeling we have when we run from danger. When we are frightened we run faster. Therefore, fear helps protect us from danger.

4. Sometimes it is better to flee and sometimes it is better to fight. Neither one is always better than the

other. Sometimes it is very smart to flee; and sometimes it is very smart to fight.

5. Anger helps you get something that you want. If it doesn't help you, then you should think about getting a substitute, changing your mind about the thing you want, or accepting the fact that you can't have what you want.

6. Hitting things is not a good way to get out anger, because it doesn't solve the main problem.

7. Holding in your anger too much can cause trouble. Letting out your anger too easily can cause trouble. The best thing is to be just in the middle.

8. Angry words let people know they are bothering you. Using good, polite angry words helps solve problems you may have with others. Using bad angry words, that is dirty words, gets people upset and usually makes things worse.

9. We cannot control our angry thoughts and angry feelings. Therefore, there is nothing to be ashamed about or to feel guilty about when we have them.

10. We can control, however, our angry acts. If you act foolishly with your angry thoughts and feelings, then you may have something to be ashamed or guilty about.

11. We cannot control our fearful thoughts and fearful feelings. Therefore, there is nothing to be ashamed about when we have them.

12. We can control our fearful acts. If we deal with them in a smart way we will have nothing to feel guilty or ashamed about.

CHAPTER 8

Love

WHAT IS LOVE?

There is no one single answer to the question: "What is love?" There are many different kinds of love. For example, there is the kind of love that grownup men and women may have for one another. I hope that your mommy and daddy have this kind of love between them. There is another kind of love that brothers and sisters often have for one another. If you have one or more brothers and sisters, I hope you have loving feelings between you. There is a kind of love that friends have for one another. I hope you have loving feelings toward your friends. But I will not be talking very much about these kinds of love in this book. I will be talking much more about the kind of love that parents can have for children and that children may have for parents. These kinds of love are most closely related to good and bad behavior, which is what this book is all about.

Mixed Feelings

It is very important to remember that love is not the only feeling that one person can have for another. Even people who love each other very much often have other feelings mixed in as well, feelings that may be different from and even opposite to love. Even when people love each other very much there are, at times, angry feelings. And, once in a while, these angry feelings may grow to be so big that one could say that hateful feelings are felt at that time. Sometimes there may be scary feelings mixed in with the loving feelings. All this is normal. When we say we love someone we really mean that the loving feelings are the most important ones. When these other feelings come over us, there is less love at that time. I am not saying that there is **no** love at that time; I am only saying that there is **less** love.

The Sun and the Clouds

Another way of understanding love is to think about the sun and the clouds. Love is like the sun. It can be bright and warm and make you feel very good. However, when people get angry or do things to one another that causes pain, the loving feelings can get less. These other things that make love less are like the clouds. They cover up the sun and make it dimmer.

The sun is still there, but you can't see it as well because these other troubles cover it up. Scary and angry feelings can do this.

Love Is Like a Light Dimmer

Most of you, I am sure, know what a light dimmer is. It's not the kind of light switch that you move up and down to make the light go on and off quickly. Rather, it's a kind of light switch that you turn in a circle, which slowly makes the light go brighter or dimmer. Usually, a dimmer switch can make the light go anywhere from completely off, to very low and dim light, to medium bright, to very bright. The love between people is very much like a light dimmer. When things are going well between the two of them, when they are happy with one another, the loving feelings may be very strong—just like when the light dimmer makes the light very bright. However, when they are upset with one another, when there may be many angry and scary feelings, then the love gets dimmer. It is still there, but it is less because of these other feelings. When the people solve the problems that make them

scared or angry, the loving feelings get stronger, the other feelings get less. Then it's just like the dimmer light becoming brighter.

Love Has Many Parts

Often, love is not a simple word to understand because it has many parts. And the different kinds of love have different kinds of parts. The love of a grown-up man and woman has different kinds of things in it than the love between a brother and sister, or the love between a parent and a child. For each kind of love it is important to know about the parts. That is the best way to find out if there is any trouble with any of the parts of love. As I said before, here I will talk only about two kinds of love: the love a parent has for a child, and the love a child has for a parent. Each of these two kinds of love has many parts, and I will talk about these parts in a little while. When you started reading this chapter you probably thought love was a very simple thing. I hope you can see now that it isn't. As you read on you will learn more about what love really is. This is important to do if you are to avoid the problems that people can have who do not understand much about love.

THE LOVE BETWEEN PARENTS AND CHILDREN

Here I will talk more about this special kind of love, the love between parents and children. As I said before, different kinds of love have different kinds of parts. First, I will talk about the parts of the love between parents and children.

Warm Feelings in the Parents' Hearts

One part of this kind of love is the parents' getting good warm feelings inside their hearts when they are with the child. This is one of the reasons why we often use a picture of a heart to show the love between people. I am not saying that the parent gets the heartwarming feelings all the time; only that most of the time the parents are with the child they have these good warm feelings inside themselves. This is also the reason why we say that a person is **heartbroken** when something bad happens to a person we love. We feel a pain in our hearts at that time. And this is especially true for a parent when something bad or terrible happens to a child.

Taking Care of a Child

Another part of the love between a parent and a child is the parent's taking care of the child. The parent wants to be sure that the child eats enough of the right kinds of foods. The parent wants to be sure that the child is dressed well, is warm in cold weather and cool in hot weather. The parent wants to be sure that the child is bathed, clean, and looks well. The parent wants to be sure that the child gets enough exercise, rest, and sleep. And the parent wants to be sure that the child is healthy. Loving parents spend a lot of time thinking about these things and the younger the child, the more they think about these things.

Touching, Rubbing, and Hugging

This is another part of the love between a parent and a child. The younger the child, the more loving parents like to do these things with their children. And, of course, the younger the child the more the child enjoys this. When people do this with one another it makes them feel very good.

Sacrifice

When I use the word sacrifice I am referring to parents' willingness to give up things that are impor-

tant to them for the sake of the child. It has something
to do with the amount of trouble they are willing to go
to and the amount of pain they are willing to suffer for
the child. People who love one another are willing to
make such sacrifices for those they love. For example,
most parents work very hard for their money. Few are
so rich that they don't have to worry about how much
money they spend. A loving parent would generally
prefer to spend money on a relaxing vacation, but is
willing to give that up if money is needed to pay the
doctor and hospital if a child is sick. In most families,
when parents buy things for their children they cannot
then use that money to buy things for themselves.
Therefore, most parents make many sacrifices for their
children. Because they love them so much, they are
willing to make these sacrifices.

Sympathy

Another part of love is sympathy. As I have said in Chapter Five, sympathy involves sharing other people's thoughts and feelings. It involves being sad when they are sad and feeling pain when they feel pain. When a parent loves a child, a parent has much sympathy. Therefore, when children are sad about something, loving parents are sympathetic. They try to put themselves in the child's situation and to see and feel things the way the child does.

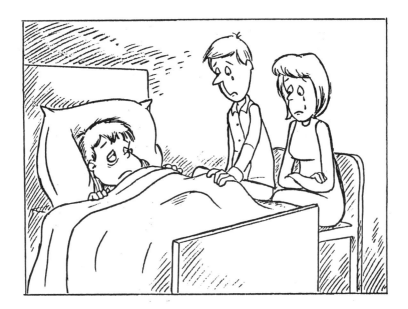

Pride

Parents who love their children are very proud of them, especially when they do things that require a lot of effort and time. For example, Mary practiced piano very hard and long. Twice a year her piano teacher had

a recital to which all the students' families were invited. At the recital her piano teacher said to Mary's parents, "She played beautifully! You should be very proud of her." Mary's parents were very proud of her and this raised her self-esteem. But, more important, Mary was very proud of herself and this raised her self-esteem even more. Her parents' pride in her accomplishment was one part of their love.

Enjoying Doing Things Together

When we love someone we enjoy doing things together with them. And this is true of parents with their children. I am not saying that parents enjoy every single minute all the time. I am only saying that when people love one another, they enjoy spending a lot of

time together. There are hundreds of different kinds of things that parents and children can do together. What they do together is less important than the fact that they are enjoying doing these things together. In some families the parents and children enjoy sports. In other families they might like hiking or going on picnics. In some families they may enjoy reading books together, listening to music, and even playing musical instruments. In other families they might play games. As I said, it is less important what you do with the people you love. It's more important that you enjoy doing things together. And this enjoyment together is part of love.

Education

Loving parents are very concerned about their children's schooling. They know it is important that their children study hard and behave properly in school. They are thinking about the future, when their children grow up and are adults. They hope that their children will learn enough to take care of themselves and earn money in order to have a family of their own someday. They know that children who have a poor education are less capable of dealing with the problems of life, both now and when they are older. Parents who worry when their children are not doing well in school are showing their love. Parents who worry when their children behave poorly in school are also showing their love.

There are some parents who do not have much love for their children. This has nothing to do with the way the children are or the way they have behaved. It's not their fault. There is something wrong with such a parent. But most children of such parents can be loved by other people. If your parent shows enough interest to read this book with you, then that parent probably has a lot of love for you. And if your parent takes care of you, makes sacrifices for you, and does the other things I just spoke about, then you can be sure that that parent loves you very much.

I hope you can see now that love is very complicated and it has many parts. I have told you here about what I consider to be the most important parts of the love of a parent for a child. There are other parts, but these are the most important to talk about for this book on children's good and bad behavior.

CHILDREN'S BEHAVIOR AND PARENTS' LOVE

As I am sure you understand, a parent's love is very important to a child. The more love a child gets from a parent, the better off the child will be. The less love a child gets from a parent, the worse off the child will be. Good behavior makes parents more loving, and they are then more likely to give the child the things I have just talked about—things like pride, sacrifice, and touching. However, bad behavior lessens the parents' loving feelings, and the child is likely to get fewer of the kinds of things I have just talked about, things like warm feelings in the parents' hearts, hugging, and sacrifices.

I am sure you remember how I compared loving feelings to a light dimmer. If you do bad things you will lessen the bright light of love that your parents have for you and you will get fewer of the things that I have just described, things like pride in you and wanting to spend a lot of time with you. I hope, therefore, that you will remember that this may happen—what consequences there will be—when you are being impulsive and ready to do bad things.

I hope you remember, as well, what I said before about how bad behavior can be like a cloud that passes over the sun and makes the sky darker. The love is still there, but it is less. I hope you will think about this when you think about doing the wrong thing, because then you will get less of the love that your parents have to give you. The important thing to remember here is that you yourself have some control over how much love you're going to get from your parents. And your behavior will determine this. I am not saying that **all** the love parents can give is related to what a child does; only **some** of it. Some parents have less to give than others. This is **not** the child's fault. I am only saying that you can increase or decrease the amount you get by your own behavior.

PARENTS' LOVE, CHILDREN'S BEHAVIOR, AND SELF-ESTEEM

I hope you remember what I said before about loving parents' having pride in their children. I spoke about Mary's parents who were very proud that she was a very good piano player. However, this is only one of thousands of things that parents could be proud of.

Parents can also be proud of a child's behavior. When children are good, parents are proud of them and will often boast to other people about how good their children have been. The children then feel high self-esteem. However, when children are bad, their parents lose pride, and the children will then feel ashamed of themselves. Such children will then suffer with feelings of low self-worth.

I hope you can see here the important relationship between parental love and your feelings of self-worth.

213

Here again, you have the control. If you are good, your parents will be proud of you and your self-worth will be higher. And if you are bad, your parents will not be proud of you, and your self-worth will be lower. It's all up to you!

PARENTAL LOVE AND VEGETABLES

You are probably wondering what parental love has to do with vegetables. You are probably saying that it has nothing at all to do with vegetables, and that there must be something wrong with me for saying that it does. Let me explain.

A vegetable just sits there. It does absolutely nothing. It doesn't move and it doesn't say anything. It doesn't even grow anymore after it has been cut from the vine or pulled out from the ground. I am sure you will agree that there isn't very much to love about a vegetable. You may think it looks nice sitting there, and may enjoy eating it, but that's not the same as loving it.

In order to get love one must do things and say things. You can't just get love by sitting there doing nothing, being like a vegetable. You must behave in a way that will bring about loving feelings in others. You must do and say those things that will make your parents happy with the way you are, with what you say, and with how you act. If you are friendly and kind to people, you will get more love from your parents. If you try hard in school and behave well there, you will also get more love from them.

There are some children who believe that their parents should love them even if they do nothing, and even if they are bad most or all of the time. I do not agree. There are even some parents who believe that they should love their child fully and completely—no matter how much like a vegetable that child may be. I do not agree. Even the most loving parents lose loving feelings when a child does nothing to be good or is bad.

I hope you can see now the relationship between parents' love and vegetables.

THE LOVE OF A CHILD
FOR A PARENT

The love of a child for a parent is another kind of love. It is different from the love of a parent for a child. It also changes much more as the child grows older. Generally, throughout a child's life, the love of a parent for a child has the same parts I just described. Here, I will talk about those parts of a love of a child for a parent that have to do with good and bad behavior.

Gratitude

When I use the word **gratitude** I am talking about feeling thankful for the things your parents do for you. Another way of saying this is that you feel grateful. Little babies do not have gratitude. They are not old enough to feel grateful. They do not understand about their parents' sacrifices and all the troubles that parents go to for them. We do not expect them to be thankful.

However, the older a child gets, the more capable the child is of feeling grateful. If you are old enough to read this book, you are old enough to have some feelings of gratitude. I am not saying that these should be as strong as those that a teenager might have, or those that an adult should have toward his (her) parents. I am only saying that children should be able to feel some gratitude.

The first step in gratitude is appreciating what your parents have done for you, especially all the good things they have given you. Another thing to think about is the sacrifices they have made for you. You may wonder here how you can best show your gratitude. As a child you cannot give them back the money that they have spent on you, nor can you do anything about the sacrifices they have made. The one thing you can do is to be good. Your good behavior is the best way to say "Thank you" to your parents. They do not expect you to give back the money, nor do they expect you to talk about how deeply you feel about their sacrifices. Many parents feel that children who behave badly show no gratitude. I am in agreement with them.

216

Thoughtfulness

One way a child can show love for a parent is thoughtfulness. When I say **thoughtfulness**, I am talking about thinking about your parents, especially thinking about things you can do that may please them. Remembering to give a parent a birthday present shows thoughtfulness. Telling your parent how sad you are when something bad happens to a parent, is also a way of showing thoughtfulness. Thoughtfulness is like sympathy, except that thoughtfulness has more to do with thoughts and sympathy has more to do with feelings. Very young children cannot be very thoughtful. They cannot put themselves in their parents' positions. If you are old enough to read this book, you are certainly old enough to be thoughtful with your parents. If you are thoughtful they will see how loving you are and they will be more loving toward you.

Sympathy

Little babies have no ability to feel sympathy. They cannot feel the same feelings their parents have. As children grow older they are more and more capable of feeling sympathy. If you are old enough to read this book, you are old enough to have some feelings of sympathy. You are old enough to be able to put yourself into another person's position, and you are old enough to feel some of the same feelings that other people feel. I am not saying that you should be able to do this as well as a teenager or an adult. I am only saying that you should be able to do this much more than a little baby.

Being sympathetic is one kind of good behavior. When something happens to a parent that makes the parent sad, it makes the parent feel better when you are sympathetic.

One Saturday morning Philip's mother got sick. She had fever, an upset stomach, and had to stay in bed. It was clear to Philip that she was miserable. He felt sorry for her. In order to make her feel better, he brought her some juice and soup. He did this to surprise her. When he came in with the tray Philip's

mother was surprised and very happy. She said: "I'm a very lucky mother to have such a kind child. My sickness is making me feel terrible. But your coming in here with this surprise has made me feel much better. I'm a very lucky mother to have a son like you."

Philip showed his loving feelings toward his mother. And what she said to him because of his good behavior made him feel very proud of himself and raised his self-esteem.

Guilt

As I said earlier in this book, younger children are not able to feel guilt. If you are old enough to read this book, you are old enough to feel guilt. You may not be able to feel as much guilt as a teenager or an adult, but you are certainly able to feel far more guilt than a little baby. Children who feel no guilt about their bad behavior make their parents very sad. Their parents lose hope that their children will ever behave well and this makes them very sad. Their loving feelings toward their children are therefore lessened. Children who feel guilty about their bad behavior—and who tell their parents about their guilt—give their parents hope that their behavior will improve. Their parents are given hope that the children will behave better and this causes them to have stronger loving feelings toward their children. Therefore, feeling guilty about bad behavior, and telling your parents about it, is one way of showing your love for them.

LOVE GROWING AND
LOVE SHRINKING

When one person loves another, and the other person loves back, the two loves together grow. However, if one person loves another and the other person doesn't love back, the first person's love will shrink. That's the way love is. To get love to increase you have to do things about it to make it increase. And this is true of the two kinds of love I've talked about here: the love of a parent for a child and the love of a child for a parent. When a child shows loving feelings toward parents, the parents' love toward the child increases. When a child shows hateful feelings toward parents and is bad, the parents' loving feelings decrease. And the same is true if the child does nothing, that is, acts like a vegetable.

IMPORTANT THINGS TO REMEMBER

1. Love is not a simple word to understand. It has many parts. Also, there are many different kinds of love.

2. When you are good your self-esteem goes higher. When you are good your parents love you even more and your self-esteem gets even higher. When you are bad your self-esteem goes lower. And when you are bad your parents love you less and your self-esteem goes even lower.

3. Your parents love for you is like the sun. When you are good there are no clouds around it and you get all the sunlight. When you are bad the clouds cover the sun and so you get less of their love.

4. Love is also like a light dimmer. When you are good the lights go up and you get more love. When you are bad the lights go down and you get less love.

5. Some parents have more love to give than others. It is **not** a child's fault if a parent has little love to give. But your behavior can increase or decrease the amount of love you get, no matter how little or how much love the parent has to start with.

I wrote this book because I want to help children have happier childhoods. Children who behave well are usually happier. Happier children grow into happier adults. And the more happy adults there are, the better will be the world in which we live.